This book was **donated** to us.
Please treat it as the **gift** it is.
"Literature is my utopia."
~ Helen Keller

KENTUCKY CLAY

Eleven Generations
of a Southern Dynasty

KATHERINE BATEMAN

CHICAGO
REVIEW
PRESS

Library of Congress Cataloging-in-Publication Data

Bateman, Katherine Roberta.

Kentucky Clay : eleven generations of a southern dynasty / Katherine
Bateman.—1st ed.

p. cm.

Includes bibliographical references and index.

ISBN-13: 978-1-55652-795-1

ISBN-10: 1-55652-795-0

1. Clay family. 2. Cecil family. 3. Kentucky—History—Biography.
4. Virginia—History—Biography. 5. Maryland—History—Biography.
6. Women—Kentucky—Biography. 7. Women—Virginia—Biography.
8. Women—Maryland—Biography. 9. Women—United States—Social
conditions. 10. Sex role—United States—History. I. Title.

CT274.C57B37 2008
975'.03092—dc22

2008009479

www.kentuckyclay.com

Interior design: Monica Baziuk

Photos courtesy of the author. Image of Kizzie Clay's house in Prestonsburg,
Kentucky, is from *Scenic South* magazine. Every effort has been made to
contact copyright holder. The editors would welcome information concerning
any inadvertent errors or omissions.

© 2009 by Katherine Bateman
All rights reserved
First Edition
Published by Chicago Review Press, Incorporated
814 North Franklin Street
Chicago, Illinois 60610
ISBN 978-1-55652-795-1
Printed in the United States of America

5 4 3 2 1

This book is dedicated
—looking back—
to all the Clay and Cecil mothers
and
—looking forward—
to my three children,
T., Lindsay, and Margret,
and to their children
and theirs

Soules they are made of Heavenly spirit:

From whence they come ye heavens inherite.

But know that body is made of Claye:

Death will devour by night and daye,

Yett is her as her was, I saye:

Ye livinge and dead remayneth Claye:

His very name that nature gave;

Is now as shall be in his grave:

Tymes doth teache, experience tyes:

That Claye to duste the winde undryes:

Then this a wonder count we must;

That want of winde should make Claye dust.

—EPITAPH FOR JOHN CLAYE ESQUIRE (1558–1632)
on his monument in the parish church of Crich, Wales

CONTENTS

INTRODUCTION

IN THE South, stories are the effervescence of conversation, and no stories are more gripping to an audience—relatives and strangers alike—than those about family.

Unlike in the North, where "family" means the existing family—the living, breathing family of siblings, parents, aunts, and uncles—in southern states "family" signifies something quite different. There, in those once defeated yet still proud states of the early colonizers, "family" means "the family," and "the family" means "the bloodline," and, for better or for worse, "the bloodline" charts a baby's fate from the moments of birth and baptism. In the North, it is "old money" that claims the mantle of aristocracy and breeding; in the South, it is "old name." Bloodlines determine playmates, eligible partners for marriage, children's names, family dog breeds, and china patterns. Bloodlines are a southern child's most significant birthright.

My family's strories are those of two colonizing families, stories passed down from generation to generation, stories of the

Clays of Virginia and the Cecils of Maryland. These families placed great value on bloodlines. Each could trace their lineage with proud exactness, could accurately illustrate their family trees with trunks of lineal descent, branches of siblings, twigs of cousins, and the two leader roots of ancient ancestors.

Family stories—any family's stories—have power, the power to define, the power to limit, the power to control. My family's stories are no different. They were not told simply to outline our heritage. They also were told to shape us in the familial image. This is not the typical book of ancestral stories that heralds only the adventures and accomplishments of the men in the family. It also focuses on the stories of the family's women. It examines the role these family stories—especially those about the wives and mothers—played in the life decisions made by the daughters who heard them. Stories were told to each of us for as long as there were storytellers alive to tell them. Some of us resisted their persuasive power. Many of us failed. The family story line was in our blood.

Members of my family seem to have been born genealogists long before genealogy became a popular pastime. They were vigilant about such things as muster records, marriage and death documents, land deeds. They saved receipts, letters, diaries, and prayer journals and then passed them on. They wrote the names of cousins and friends under oval-framed faces in leather-bound picture albums so the next generation—and the next after that— would not be confused about those pale images and misguidedly throw away the picture of a family member.

I have inherited these papers and albums. A muster record from the cavalry unit my great-grandfather raised for the Union during the Civil War lies at this moment on my desk. Although it has been folded and unfolded countless times, it is now flattened under a protective piece of glass. Someone in the family

—probably my mother, on whose desk it lay before mine—has strengthened the folds with tape. The tape has aged in gradations of golden molasses and is especially dark where the tape itself is beginning to curl. The sepia ink my great-grandfather preferred has faded to tan, yet I can read his name, Captain Frank Mott, written over and over as each new soldier was mustered in and then mustered out. His script is perfect. Despite the solemnity of the moment—the signing in and the signing out of that terrible war—Frank Mott has a languid hand. His letters slant toward the finish, yet do not slur or mumble. I feel I know my great-grandfather as much from this document as from the stories his daughter so lovingly told me.

The family also saved things. I inherited jewelry, fancy belt buckles, silver urns, a flayed silk parasol with a carved ivory handle. I inherited the mahogany couch my great great-grandfather sent to his wife in Prestonsburg, Kentucky, by flatboat from Frankfort, where he was serving in the legislature in 1860, and a piece of the original upholstery material that covered the couch on its way from the statehouse to the mountains. I inherited brass carriage clocks, opalescent opera glasses, wedding dresses, blue ribbons for champion trotting horses, and plates and bowls with designs in terracotta red and floe blue brought back from China during the early China trade.

None of these objects came over from England on the boats that transported my relatives—John Thomas Claye and Thomas Cecil—along with other sons from aristocratic families to the New World. Rather, they were acquired along the way by the children of those founding families in Virginia and Maryland who knew their history, who had been told about the battles their ancestors fought and the roles they played in colonizing America.

As a child I listened to these proud tales of colonization in a state of confusion. I was puzzled and, later, embarrassed by the superior tone of the storytellers. I chafed under the responsibility that came with the stories—the stated charge to remember these stories, to pass them on. I was told that the Clay and Cecil family bloodlines and the accompanying stories were as much a part of my heritage as the sterling silver tea service with each owner's initials engraved one under the other.

The stories about the Clay and Cecil women were more personal than those of the men. I learned how they supervised the farms and plantations while their husbands built their careers, ran for public office, and fought wars. Yet mostly the stories about the women were about emotional reactions, about responses to events. Their stories were about recalcitrant daughters who turned into strong-willed women, about mothers who did not enjoy the practice of mothering but with uncanny prescience married men who were unusually nurturing and loving to the children. Theirs were stories about daughters who loved their fathers more than their mothers, yet chose to be buried near their mothers rather than lie next to their husbands and children. And theirs were stories about Clay wives who divorced their husbands when divorce was still unseemly.

The Clay and Cecil women's stories were also about houses— houses with which the women in my family had obsessive and, at times, near-incestuous relationships. There were stories of houses left in moments of pique, houses burned down in spiteful anger, houses loved but sold because of great sadness experienced in their rooms. In the stories it is difficult to separate the Clay and Cecil women and their houses, difficult to tell who is taking center stage—the actor or the theater.

I was never comfortable with this talk of bloodlines, and I am not comfortable now. I did not embrace the pride I was supposed to experience because I was a Clay and a Cecil. I suspected that most of the stories my relatives chose to glorify were inflated versions of the truth. I secretly believed that the value placed on the stories was more about family self-esteem than about family history. For most of my life I ran from the stories. "You can't make a silk purse out of a sow's ear" was one of Rebecca Cecil's favorite sayings, passed down for generations before it was repeatedly quoted to me, her great-great-great-granddaughter. I did not want to be a silk purse. I did not want to be like the women in the stories. I did not want to be another unloving mother. I wanted to break the matriarchal pattern of divorce.

I do not know why I resisted the family ancestry as much as I did. My brother did not fight it. My mother and grandmother and all the women before me seemed to nestle without question into the plumped-down comfort of their once-famous family's legacy —Thomas Cecil's early map of Maryland, Henry "The Great Compromiser" Clay's campaigns for president, Cassius Marcellus "Cash" Clay's abolitionist role in Lincoln's decisions to emancipate the slaves and his reward of an ambassadorship to Russia for supporting Lincoln's presidential campaign in the first place.

I left for college when I was seventeen. I turned my back on the family's last stop on their three-hundred-fifty-year trek from the shores of Virginia and Maryland—along the James River, onto Swift Creek, across the softly rolling landscape of Virginia toward the hills that rise up in the west to blot out the afternoon sun, to the New River and the New River Valley in the Blue Ridge mountain chain, through a pass in the Alleghenies into Kentucky, down the Levisa Fork of the Big Sandy River to Prestonsburg, to Louisa, and finally to Catlettsburg, Kentucky, where the Big Sandy submits to the rush of the Ohio River. I left the northeastern sector of Kentucky, where generations of my relatives were known, and I never looked back.

At Berea College in central Kentucky I felt anonymous. No one knew I was a Clay and a Cecil. I did not disclose that my relative "Cash" Clay had donated the land for the college and had hired the abolitionist minister John G. Fee in 1850 to open the first school. I moved to Ann Arbor, Michigan, when I was twenty-one hoping to further distance myself from the family and the stories that, in that 1960s midwestern center of liberalism, seemed to me like an oppressive undertow. Soon I quit fretting over the disconnect the stories seemed to cause between my family's values and mine.

Yet now, in my sixties with children and grandchildren, I am ready to face the stories. My reason is simple. My children do not know them. I did not pass on the family history the way it had been passed to me.

There is, however, a second, far-reaching reason to remember the stories. I am embarrassed, as a historian, that it took so long for me to recognize it. I have in my possession a treasure trove of information about the way this country came together. Some of it takes physical form—muster papers, genealogy charts, photographs, letters. But more fragile and more apt to be lost is the oral history. The stories I carry in my head define one family's path through the history of this country—the land they acquired, the battles they fought, the decisions they made to move into isolated areas, and the consequences of those decisions. I know the names of neighbors, how kinship groups formed along the rivers of Virginia, how my relatives died, and what they left in their wills.

Still, I ask myself, are the stories about the women—the mothers in our family—a legacy I want to pass on? Is it possible to reveal the strength in my female relatives despite the way the stories amplify their willfulness, selfishness, and spiteful behavior? Is it enough to say that the women in the family acted as they did out of frustration? The Clay women shared a gene pool with lawyers, judges, state and national legislators, ambassadors, advisors to presidents, and a presidential candidate, yet did not have the same opportunities to be proactive as did their fathers, brothers, male cousins, and sons. Could that not explain why these women, who were educated equally with their male relatives, turned bitter, turned inward, and drank? Yet, this too—the stories of smart women left behind—is part of our country's history, is part of America's culture that is only now beginning to change.

So I will tell the stories. I will pass them on the way they were told to me. Yet I am by nature historian first and storyteller second. I have suspected all my life that the family tales were based on a pebble of fact encircled by a pond of fiction. The family antidote for any adversity has always been "Well, at least it will make a good story." It seemed only natural to me as I was growing up that all stories needed to be "good stories"—tales that exaggerated events in order to spellbind the listener.

As a historian I have worked to uncover the origin and the truth of those stories one by one, generation by generation. I was trained to examine history from the top down—from the famines and wars, from the plagues and political unrest. This time I have done my research from the roots up. I follow the Clays as they move from the rivers of the Chesapeake to the mountains of Kentucky and beyond. I understand now that the stories are my birthright, my legacy—as the storytellers always stressed. If I can tell them well, make them come alive, if I can describe the landscape and set the historic scene, maybe I can make these stories about a single family the proud legacy of us all.

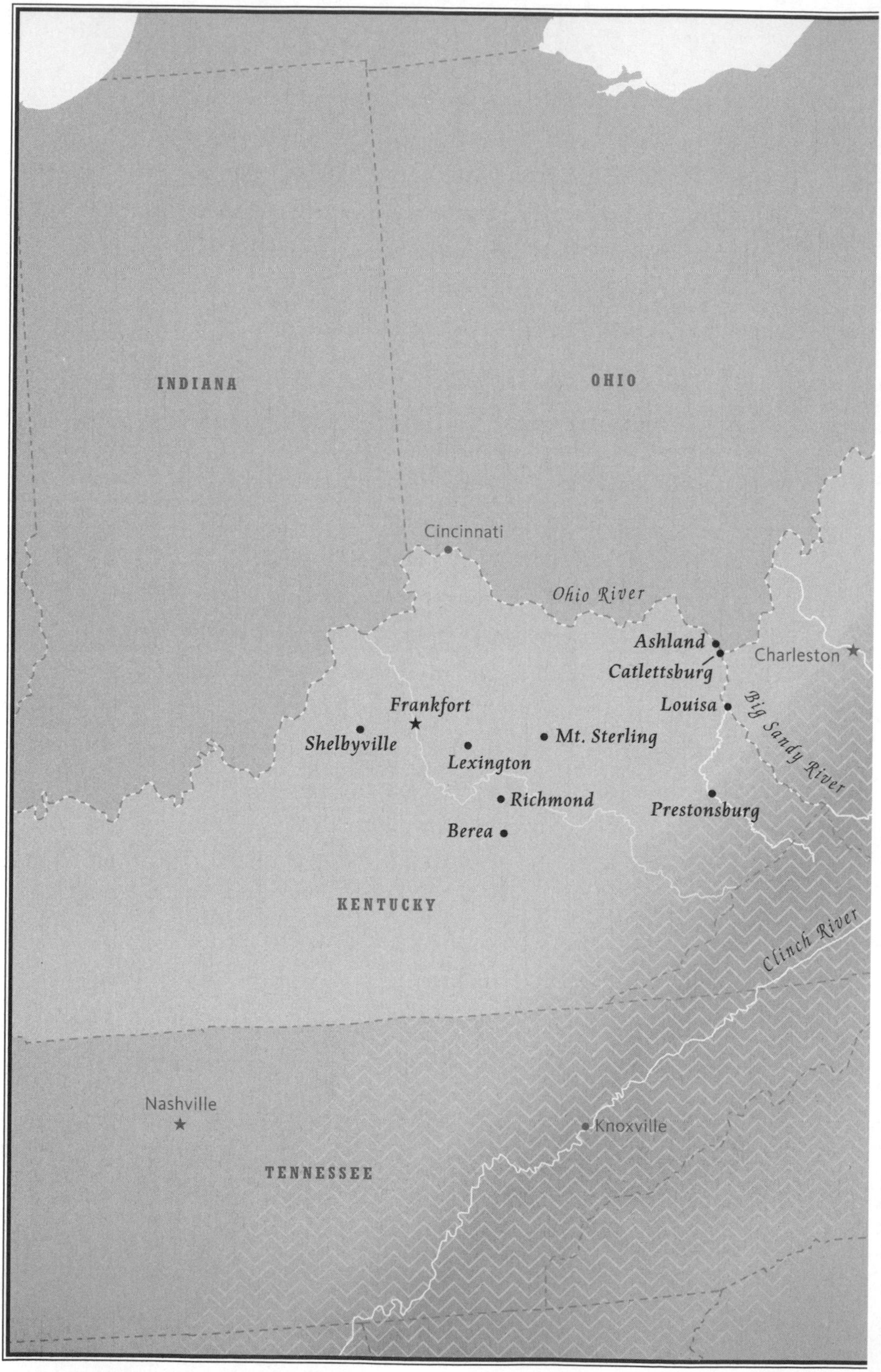

INDIANA
OHIO
Cincinnati
Ohio River
Ashland
Catlettsburg
Charleston
Louisa
Big Sandy River
Frankfort
Shelbyville
Lexington
Mt. Sterling
Richmond
Prestonsburg
Berea
KENTUCKY
Clinch River
Nashville
Knoxville
TENNESSEE

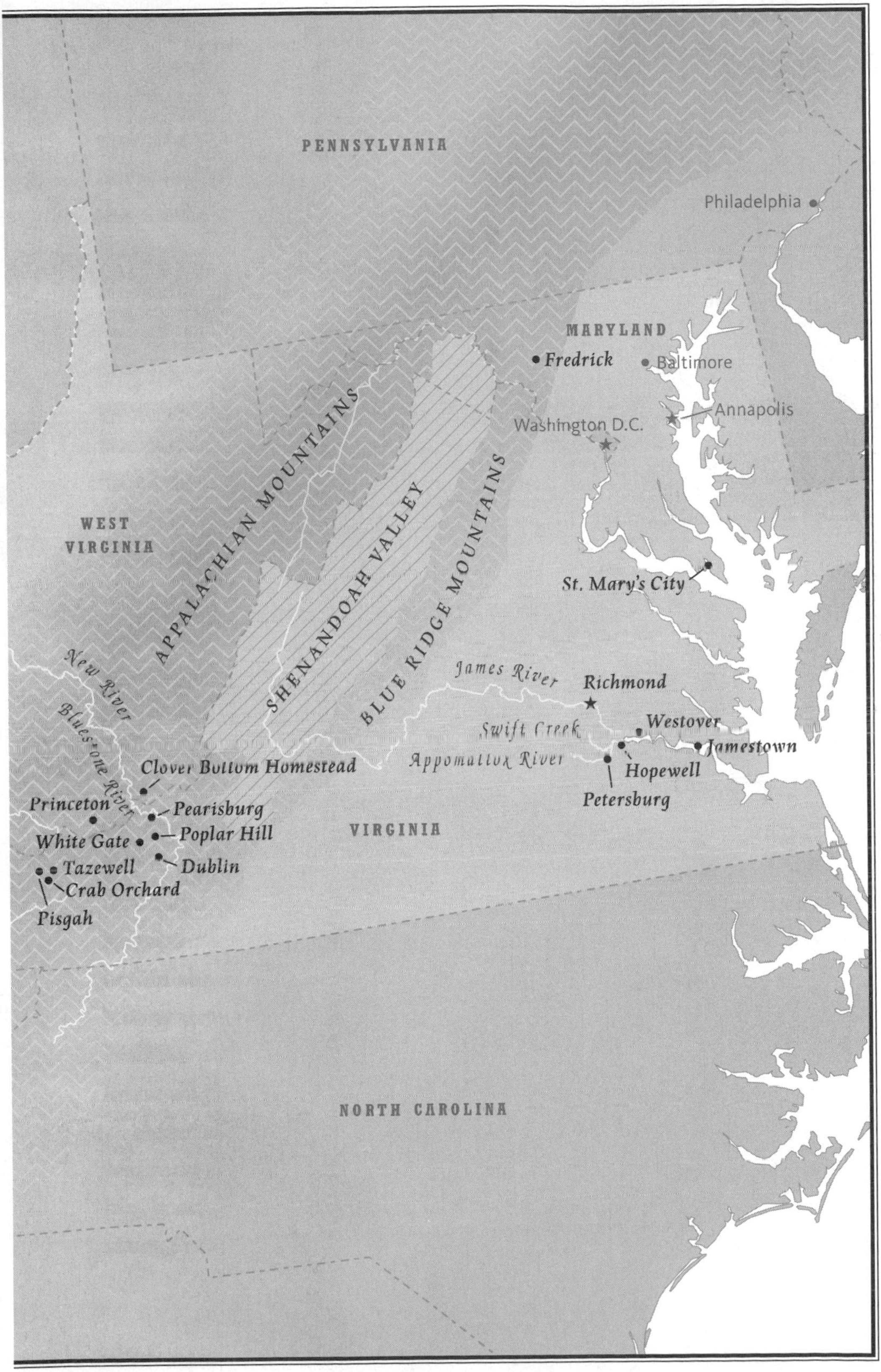
PENNSYLVANIA
Philadelphia
MARYLAND
Fredrick
Baltimore
Annapolis
Washington D.C.
APPALACHIAN MOUNTAINS
SHENANDOAH VALLEY
BLUE RIDGE MOUNTAINS
WEST VIRGINIA
St. Mary's City
New River
Bluestone River
James River
Richmond
Swift Creek
Westover
Jamestown
Appomattox River
Hopewell
Petersburg
Clover Bottom Homestead
Princeton
Pearisburg
Poplar Hill
White Gate
Dublin
Tazewell
Crab Orchard
Pisgah
VIRGINIA
NORTH CAROLINA

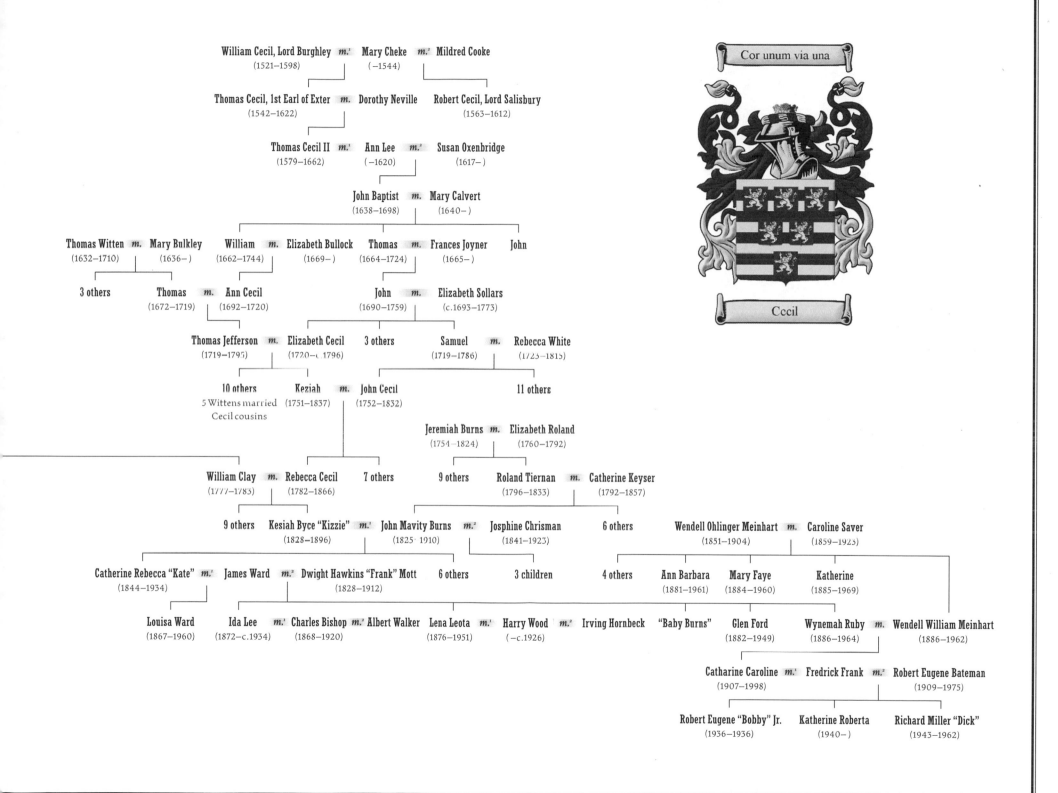

Cor unum via una

Cecil

William Cecil, Lord Burghley *m.¹* Mary Cheke *m.²* Mildred Cooke
(1521–1598) (−1544)

Thomas Cecil, 1st Earl of Exter *m.* Dorothy Neville   Robert Cecil, Lord Salisbury
(1542–1622) (1563–1612)

Thomas Cecil II *m.¹* Ann Lee *m.²* Susan Oxenbridge
(1579–1662) (−1620) (1617−)

John Baptist *m.* Mary Calvert
(1638–1698) (1640−)

Thomas Witten *m.* Mary Bulkley   William *m.* Elizabeth Bullock   Thomas *m.* Frances Joyner   John
(1632–1710) (1636−) (1662–1744) (1669−) (1664–1724) (1665−)

3 others   Thomas *m.* Ann Cecil   John *m.* Elizabeth Sollars
(1672–1719) (1692–1720) (1690–1759) (c.1693–1773)

Thomas Jefferson *m.* Elizabeth Cecil   3 others   Samuel *m.* Rebecca White
(1719–1795) (1720–c.1796) (1719–1786) (1723–1815)

10 others   Keziah *m.* John Cecil   11 others
5 Wittens married   (1751–1837) (1752–1832)
Cecil cousins

Jeremiah Burns *m.* Elizabeth Roland
(1754–1824) (1760–1792)

William Clay *m.* Rebecca Cecil   7 others   9 others   Roland Tiernan *m.* Catherine Keyser
(1777–1783) (1782–1866) (1796–1833) (1792–1857)

9 others   Kesiah Byce "Kizzie" *m.¹* John Mavity Burns *m.²* Josphine Chrisman   6 others   Wendell Ohlinger Meinhart *m.* Caroline Saver
(1828–1896) (1825–1910) (1841–1923) (1851–1904) (1859–1923)

Catherine Rebecca "Kate" *m.¹* James Ward *m.²* Dwight Hawkins "Frank" Mott   6 others   3 children   4 others   Ann Barbara   Mary Faye   Katherine
(1844–1934) (1828–1912) (1881–1961) (1884–1960) (1885–1969)

Louisa Ward   Ida Lee *m.¹* Charles Bishop *m.²* Albert Walker   Lena Leota *m.¹* Harry Wood *m.²* Irving Hornbeck   "Baby Burns"   Glen Ford   Wynemah Ruby *m.* Wendell William Meinhart
(1867–1960) (1872–c.1934) (1868–1920) (1876–1951) (−c.1926) (1882–1949) (1886–1964) (1886–1962)

Catharine Caroline *m.¹* Fredrick Frank *m.²* Robert Eugene Bateman
(1907–1998) (1909–1975)

Robert Eugene "Bobby" Jr.   Katherine Roberta   Richard Miller "Dick"
(1936–1936) (1940−) (1943–1962)

1

THE ANCIENT PLANTER

ALTHOUGH I cannot prove it, I am convinced that John Thomas Claye—the first of my ancestors to come over from England —had brown eyes. This may sound odd, even inconsequential to families who over time have looked into the eyes of relatives that reflect rainbow hues: blue, green, violet, or that luscious yellow that turns to key lime in certain lights. It is not odd, however, to me. My conviction that John Thomas Claye had brown eyes has substance behind it.

All of us, all of the Clays and Cecils—the mothers, the fathers, the sisters, the brothers, the grandparents, the babies— are brown-eyed. Photographs show our dark chocolate eyes for the seven generations that cameras have existed to capture them. Histories of the early settlers of Virginia and Kentucky go even further back. One author speaks of my eighteenth-century relatives not just in terms of their Revolutionary War service or their careers in law and politics but also discusses in surprisingly lush language the family's dark brunette looks. A husband writes love letters to "my black-eyed baby." Oral tradition describes "black eyes flashing."

Consequently, I think that when John Thomas Claye sailed into the Chesapeake Bay in February 1613 he gazed at his new Virginia homeland through irises of brown. I think his dark eyes darkened further when he stepped off the ship *Treasurer* onto the wharf built just months before on the James River side of the fledgling Jamestown colony. They darkened in stunned disbelief as he walked through the palisade and took in the handful of crude shelters, the deep mud, and the lethargic shamble of the Jamestown colonists who, like him, had invested as land speculators in "The Tresorer and Companie of Adventurers and Planters of the Citty of London for the Firste Colonie in Virginia."

Imagining John Thomas's brown eyes as he stares in confused shock at the skeletal colonists—the ones who felt lucky to have survived "the starving years" of 1609 to 1611—helps me feel that I am in that rain-drenched Jamestown winter with him. I stand beside him as he surveys the bleak and dreary settlement he has come to: the two rows of timber and mud houses, the disheveled storehouses within the fort's triangular form shaped by precariously leaning palisades. I stand there as he contrasts the noisy vibrancy of London—the home he had left just weeks before—with the sluggish stillness of this exhausted place. I want to comfort this twenty-six-year-old relative of mine as he wonders if the *Treasurer* has docked too soon, as he tells himself this must not be the Jamestown he was promised, the place he has invested in, the place where he plans to buy land, make a home, start a family.

Yes, I want to comfort him. I want to touch his arm. I want to say to John Thomas, "Look at me. Look at my brown eyes. I am one of yours. Eleven generations of your family know your story. Your story and all those like yours taught us what we can do, who we can be. We know that so many of you faced this awful place alone and that you did not give up, you did not go back to the safety, the familiarity of England. Through your stories we know we are capable of taking risks, capable of starting over; we know we are capable of change. We owe the first step in family fearlessness to you. So many of us are here to affirm that the decision each of you made was a positive one, not just for you but for all of us in your bloodlines."

According to the family story, John Thomas Claye came to Virginia in 1613 for one reason only: to amass land. He made that trip across the Atlantic on the ship *Treasurer* in the dangerous gray winter seas to replace the land he would have inherited if he had not been born the second son of Sir John Thomas Claye and Mary Carleton Claye, if England's laws of primogeniture had not determined that his older brother, William, would get everything. To match the family landholdings was a tall order. The Clayes were well established in England. John Thomas's father was a Welsh coal baron knighted by Elizabeth I, and his mother was the daughter of Sir William Carlton, the "Chief Cockmatcher and Servant to the Hawks" for Henry VIII.

At first, John Thomas had not considered buying stock in "The Tresorer and Companie of Adventurers and Planters of the Citty of London for the Firste Colonie in Virginia" or sailing to Jamestown. For one thing, he had not reached his majority in 1606 when the "Virginia Company" put out its first call for adventurers to participate "in purse or in person" in the land investment venture. And then ships filled with additional adventurers and supplies for the fledgling colony began to return to London with more than logs and furs. The ships also returned with stories. Hard-to-believe stories. Stories the board members of the Virginia Company tried to hide, with little success, from the public. Potential stockholders clustered in London's business district and conferred over what they had heard from the captains and crew of the ships returning from Virginia. In spring 1608, only thirty-six of the first one hundred fifty adventurers survived the first year in the new colony. Could this be true? In 1610, of the five hundred settlers in the colony in 1608—most healthy new adventurers—only sixty were still alive. And, nearly unspeakably, those sixty may have survived only because they were willing to eat their own dead. Unthinkable.

At first, John Thomas Claye was not tempted to join the sons of English nobility in the Virginia Company venture: at first, the second sons who trickled into the fledgling colony and, later, the "distressed cavaliers" who flooded into Virginia in the 1640s following their land losses in the English Civil War. John Thomas was not interested in Jamestown until 1612. That spring, news of an amazing new strain of tobacco reached London, tobacco planted in Virginia from Spanish seeds acquired in the West Indies by John Rolfe, an early Virginia Company adventurer and future husband of Pocahontas. This tobacco was so wondrous that descriptions of its luscious leaves—their resistance to disease, their richness of flavor—reached London before the first hogshead filled with the precious commodity left Virginia a year or more later. The news of this fine new cash crop was all it took to rekindle interest in the Virginia colony and to pique John Thomas's interest.

The Virginia Company seized the moment. On March 12, 1612, the stock company rewrote its charter to extend the boundaries of the Virginia settlements one hundred miles west to allow for large tobacco plantations. Flyers to entice new investors passed from hand to hand. Pay your own way: get a grant of one hundred acres of river-rich plantation land. Private men's clubs were full of the talk of this amazing new tobacco, of the land that could be had, the money that could be made in the new world.

So in 1612, while the hubbub raged about Virginia's new cash crop, John Thomas Claye, now twenty-six and still single, thought about the land in England lost to birth order. As I imagine it, he considered the thousands of acres of available land in Virginia. He pictured the family's land in mountainous Monmouth, Wales. He tried to imagine the flat but fertile marshland described by those who had returned from Virginia. He mulled his future over and over, looking this way and that at the idea of emigrating to Virginia. And finally he came to the conclusion that the only way to have the life he wanted was to join the swell of second sons sailing to Virginia. He joined forces with the Virginia Company, purchased a fare on the ship *Treasurer,* and sailed to Virginia "in purse" and "in person" to amass land as a planter.

The first decision John Thomas Claye made after arriving in wet, dreary Jamestown set a precedent for generations of our family. John Thomas decided to move away from the more established settlements in the colony. For his initial grant of one hundred acres he chose a site near present-day Hopewell on the south side of the James River, about twenty miles west of James-town in newly laid out Charles City County. The land—taken from the Appomattocs in the winter of 1611–12—was fertile. It was so fertile, in fact, that it was named the "new Bermuda" after the lush soil of the Bermuda Islands. Further, it was near choice transportation routes. To the north of John Thomas's patent was the James River. To his west the wide mouth of the Appomattox River flowed into the James, commingled with the many fingers of Swift Creek. Further, there were large tracts of land in Charles City County, space for bigger plantations. John Thomas planted his first crop of tobacco in spring 1613 and began to acquire land near his plantation.

Life was not easy. Although, according to the muster records, two of John Thomas's shipmates from the *Treasurer*—Christopher Safford and Henry Williams—settled near him, it was a lonely time. In 1616, three years after John Thomas made his claim, John Rolfe sent a formal letter to the Virginia Company entitled "A True Relation of the State of Virginia." In it he spoke to the plight of planters like John Thomas and asked for financial rewards and enticements for the colony:

> The number of Officers and Laborers are 205. The Farmers 81. besides 65 woemen and children in every place some, which in all amounteth to 351 persons: a small number to advaunce so greate a worke.

Rolfe's plea for help struck a responsive chord in England. That year, 1616, the Virginia Company decided to expand its rewards to colonizers by speeding up the receipt of land grants. Any planter who had come to Virginia before 1616—"the ancient planters"—would receive one hundred acres effective 1619 as long as they, like John Thomas, had been in Virginia for three years. Further, for each person whose fare was paid to the Company by an adventurer, the transporter would receive fifty additional acres.

The new land rewards worked in John Thomas's favor. In May 1619 John Thomas paid for the passage of his servant William Nicholls to come over on the ship *Dutie.* Over the next thirteen years he paid the passages of twenty-one additional adventurers and planters—some of whom most likely worked off their debt to John Thomas on his plantations. In 1635 John Thomas received a patent on eleven hundred acres, which gave him the right to land that lay adjacent to his original one-hundred-acre grant—acreage that now stretched between Ward's Creek and Bailey's Creek on the south side of the James River just below the mouth of the Appomattox River. By the time he died he owned thousands of acres of plantation land on both sides of the James River.

John Thomas Claye's journey to Virginia was part of each Clay child's history. We knew his story. We knew him by his double first name, John Thomas. We knew that at some point he left that strange "e" off the end of his name. And we knew that our cousin Green Clay—who wrote down a record of the Clay family in the nineteenth century—called John Thomas "the English Grenadier." We also knew that in April 1623 he brought over Ann Nichols on the ship *Ann*. According to the family saga, John Thomas had married Ann Nichols sometime before he made his decision to go to Virginia. Others who have researched the Clays suggest they married later. There is no documentation to prove either account. All we know is that in 1624 Ann was in Virginia and claimed to have arrived on the ship *Ann* the year before.

In 1624 a census was taken of the Virginia colony inhabitants. At that time John Thomas Claye and Ann Nichols Claye lived in Jordans Journey Charles Cittie. On January 21, 1624, when the census taker reached their plantation, John Thomas and Ann Nichols had one servant—William Nicholls—thirty bushels of corn, one hundred fish, two cows, one pig, ten chickens, various armaments, and one house. But the census record of John's fish and chickens was not important to the family version of John Thomas's story. Nor in John Thomas's story were there imaginings of a first makeshift dwelling, of a later log cabin, of a final home with outbuildings for curing tobacco, for livestock, for storage. What was important to the chroniclers of the family saga was this: John Thomas Claye came to Virginia to replace land lost to English laws, and he met his goal. He purchased land, sold land, and purchased more. He received land grants and formed land partnerships. John Thomas Claye came here land poor and died land rich.

Each of the young Clay listeners attached images to John Thomas's tale. Mine were as I described in the beginning. As I learned about Jamestown in grade school I pictured John Thomas's arrival in that dank, muddy place called a colony. I sensed his start of apprehension as he looked out across the wharf toward the hovels serving as homes. I saw his dark eyes widen as he stared at the starving, lumbering wraiths who inhabited this ring of Dante's hell. I was certain he questioned his decision to leave England, certain that he wondered if he had made a terrible mistake. I was convinced that he asked himself if he had the will to do what he had set out to do.

John Thomas Claye's story ended well. He had his land. He fathered a family who would follow his lead—children and grandchildren and their children and grandchildren who would survey land and move west and south and west again toward the dangerous edges of this country's expansion, toward larger landholdings, toward long, languorous vistas, toward fresh but fearsome new starts. John Thomas died at age sixty-eight in 1655, and because primogeniture did not cross the Atlantic with the second sons of nobility, each of his children—sons all—inherited a land stake of his own with enough left over to pass down.

And what of the women in John Thomas's life? He had married twice. Ann Nichols, his first wife, had only a walk-on part in his story—a marriage date, a muster record, three sons: William, Francis, and Thomas. I had thought little about Ann Nichols Claye before I made the decision to delve into the family history.

In my research I discovered that Ann had arrived in Virginia at a treacherous time.

On March 22, 1622, Opechancanough, Pocahontas's uncle, out of frustration that the English were in Virginia to stay, staged synchronized, surprise early morning attacks on settlements up and down the James River. Three hundred forty-seven settlers were shot or hacked to death in their homes and fields. John Thomas Claye and William Nicholls were among the few who survived the raids. Less than a year later—while a consortium of Indian tribes were desperately trying to drive the English into the Chesapeake Bay—Ann Nichols boarded the ship *Ann* for Virginia.

Why did John Thomas ask Ann to come to Virginia during that unsettled period? By summer 1622, news of the "great Massacre" had reached London and was circulating around England. Recruitment was difficult. But Ann Nichols came on. Did John Thomas think that moving to the fortress at Jordan's Journey— where the surviving settlers of the plantations in the Bermuda Hundred had been directed to converge—made it safe? There is no way to know the answer, yet Ann Nichols did survive the years of unrest in the 1620s. She died sometime before 1645, some twenty years after her arrival in Virginia. There are few family stories about John Thomas and Ann Nichols's three boys, born during those early, difficult colonizing years. John Thomas's youngest son, Charles Clay, the child of his marriage to his second wife, Elizabeth, however, did hold importance to the family. He was our direct lineal relative and the great-great-great-grandfather of Henry Clay, the Kentucky statesman and presidential contender and one of the family's great prides.

2

THE CHYRURGIEN
AND THE REBEL

CHARLES CLAY had only two reference points in the family saga: he was John Thomas Claye's youngest child, and he fought in Bacon's Rebellion—a fact that amused and confused me as a child since I heard the stories in word pictures. I wanted to know more about Charles than those two meager crumbs of information. I wanted him to come alive for me. I had stood in my imagination with his father when he faced desolate Jamestown. I wanted to stand beside Charles for at least a moment of his life. So I headed to Chicago's Newberry Library—a noted research center for early American history.

First I researched Charles Clay's birth. The family's genealogy chart said Charles was born in 1638 and was the child of Ann Nichols. Neither of these facts fit with the documents I uncovered in Virginia's court records. Finally, I found a deposition that Charles gave on October 2, 1682, where he stated that he was "about 37 years old." That meant he was born in 1645. Ann Nichols had died by then. His mother had to be John Thomas's second wife, Elizabeth, whose maiden name remains a mystery.

Corroboration for Elizabeth as Charles Clay's birth mother came from a surprising source: Elizabeth's second husband. Following John Thomas's death in 1655, Elizabeth married her neighbor, John Wall, who in 1629 had patented land adjacent to property owned by John Thomas on the mouth of Ward's Creek. On October 3, 1660, John Wall recorded a deeded gift of two ewes made to Charles, "his sonne-in-law"—seventeenth-century usage for stepson. That cinched it. Elizabeth Wall, formerly Elizabeth Claye, was Charles Clay's mother. She—not Ann Nichols—was my great-great-great-great-great-great-great-great-grandmother.

Next I discovered a document that began to flesh out the story line of this obscure relative of mine. It seems that Charles had chosen a career quite different from that of his father. Rather than being a planter and land speculator, Charles wanted to be a "chyrurgien." In 1657, two years after John Thomas Claye died and with his stepfather's help, Charles, age twelve, apprenticed himself to Stephen Tickner, a surgeon in Surry County. Tickner was to "imploy him aboute in the way of Chyrurgerye, or Phisick, for & duringe the terme and time of seaven yeares." Tickner agreed "to use his best skill & Judgmt. to learne him his Art." He also agreed that "what cloathes the sd. Charles doth bring, the sd. Tickner is to returne to him at the Expiration of the time affords."

Charles Clay signed the indenture for his seven years of training on October 10, 1657. It was witnessed by Dan Veale, who signed with his mark, and by Charles's stepfather, John Wall. I could begin to see Charles, see him learning a trade, growing taller year by year. I could picture him toward the end of his

apprenticeship. He was a young man now, fully grown. I could
see him in a small log structure with rough-hewn shelves for the
tools of his new trade—the jars of leeches, the knives, the pliers,
the wooden chair, the bottle of corn liquor. Then I saw him bun-
dle up the "cloathes" he had come with, the clothes that marked
his growth over the last seven years, saw him climbing on a river
transport in Surry County, Virginia, to return upriver to Henrico
County where he had grown up.

It was 1664. He was nearly twenty. He went home to court
Hannah Wilson. Hannah Wilson, like Ann Nichols, was only
a name in the family litany of ancestors. Yet, in my attempt to
catch at least a glimpse of Charles's adult life, an interesting thing
happened. I found I could more easily relate to my great-great-
great-great-great-great-great-grandmother, Hannah Wilson
Clay, than I could to Charles.

Hannah was the daughter of Hannah James and John Wilson Senior, who emigrated to Virginia in 1623. John Wilson, like
John Thomas, had chosen to patent land on the far western edge
of the Virginia colony and purchased land on the north side of
the Appomattox River on the second falls of Swift Creek. Both
Hannah and Charles belonged to the first generation of "adventurer" children to be born in the Virginia colony. Hannah knew
about on-again, off-again relations with the Indians. She knew
about life on the frontier. So it seemed natural to me that she and
Charles Clay should wed in 1667 and begin to have children—two
daughters and then four sons and finally another daughter. Then,
in the midst of her childbearing years, Hannah had to deal with
Charles's near-fatal alliance with his and Hannah's new neighbor
Nathaniel Bacon, the future leader of Bacon's Rebellion. Charles
was twenty-nine, Nathaniel twenty-seven when they met. Two
years passed before the association turned dangerous.

Before I go further, I have to admit that prior to researching Charles Clay I knew nothing about Bacon's Rebellion except that one of my relatives had fought in it. My academic background is in early medieval English and European history. Although I have been teaching myself American history over the last two decades, learning about Bacon's Rebellion was not at the top of my list—not until I decided to reacquaint myself with my own family's history. So in trying to piece together a life for Charles Clay I realized I had to understand what Bacon's Rebellion was about and how Charles got involved.

Picture the backdrop for the rebellion that is about to unfold. The year is 1676. Verdant Virginia forests and farmland stretch out as far as you can see. The countryside is engraved by the slow darkish curves of the James and Appomattox rivers as they snake back and forth, north and south, yet always west, away from the older settlements to the east. In summer the lush green landscape is dotted with the caramel-colored leaves of tobacco plants, leaves that age to corn silk bronze before they are stripped from their stalks and hauled to drying barns. New settlers arrive steadily to claim land in the frontier regions that follow the river into what is now Richmond. And so, in this lush setting, the story of Bacon's Rebellion, the first of the country's uprisings against the Crown, begins.

The sparking reason for Bacon's Rebellion was colonist taxation without Crown protection. In the spring of 1676, Indian attacks on the planters on Virginia's western frontier were increasing in fervor and frequency—livestock killed, crops destroyed, families murdered. In response to a request from the planters for help, Virginia's Crown-appointed governor, William Berkeley, made a decision that nearly cost him his life and in the end cost him his job. Instead of sending troops to protect the colonists, whose

heavy taxes helped maintain a military presence for this very purpose, Governor Berkeley chose to cut off all fur trade between
the settlers and the Indians until tempers cooled down. Settlers seethed. Profits were lost and families left unprotected. The
frontier settlers decided to take matters into their own hands.
Nathaniel Bacon, new to the colony, was quick to offer his ser-
vices as their leader.

Nathaniel Bacon was no George Washington. He had arrived
in Virginia on a tobacco ship in 1674. He had a past of personal
insurrections. His father, Thomas Bacon, had tired of his son's
"extravagancies" and shipped him off with eighteen hundred
pounds sterling to start a new life in the colonies. With Bacon
traveled his young wife, Elizabeth Duke, who had been disin-
herited when her father discovered that she had secretly married
Bacon.

Bacon was twenty-seven when he arrived in the colony. He
almost immediately purchased frontier land in Henrico County
on the north side of the James River near the plantation Westover. Hannah and Charles Clay lived in Westover Parish on land
John Thomas had purchased around 1636. Bacon—who had been
described by his tutor at Cambridge University as of "very good
parts, and a quick wit [though] impatient of labour"—made
friends easily.

Because I know that historians—no matter how objective we
endeavor to be—cannot escape our personal biases, I prefer to
study events through primary sources, through letters, notebooks,
diaries, journals. Consequently, I searched for a mid-seventeenth-
century document that would lift me in real time and language
patterns into Charles and Hannah's lives. I could not believe my
good fortune when I came across a letter written on Saturday,
June 29, 1676, by Elizabeth Duke, Nathaniel Bacon's young wife

and Hannah and Charles's neighbor—a letter Elizabeth wrote to her sister in England.

In this letter Elizabeth described the events of the spring and summer of Bacon's Rebellion in such detail that as I read word after word I was transported back. I was there on the frontier plantations in Westover Parish on the north bank of the James River with Hannah and Elizabeth as they suffered through that hot, fearsome summer of 1676. I was there as they worried about the crops and the livestock and their own safety. I was there and I was angry. I was angry at Nathaniel Bacon for being a shallow boy-man with a deep-seated need to hold power, and I was angry at Charles Clay for not seeing Bacon for what he was and for falling—along with 209 others—under his destructive charismatic spell.

Here is how Elizabeth tells the story of Bacon's Rebellion.

Dear Sister,

I pray God keep the Worst Enemy I have from ever being in such a sad condition as I have been in since my former to the [unreadable] occasioned by ye troublesome Indians, who have killed one of our overseers at an outward plantation which wee had, and wee have lost a great stock of cattle, which wee had upon it, and a good crop that wee should have made there, such plantations Nobody durst come nigh, which is a very great losse to us.

If you had been here, it would have grieved your heart to hear the pitiful complaints of the people, the Indians killing the people daily the Govern not taking any notice of it for to hinder them, but let them daily doe all the mischief they can. I am sure if the Indians were not cowards, they might have destroyed all the upper plantations, and killed all the people upon them; the Governour so much their friend, that hee would not suffer any body to hurt one of the

Indians; and the poor people came to your brother to desire him to
help against the Indians, and hee being very much concerned for the
losse of his Overseer, and for the losse of so many men and women
and children's lives every day, hee was willing to doe them all the
good hee could; so he begged of the Governour for a commission in
severall letters to him, that hee might goe out against them, but hee
would not grant one . . .

Despite the denial of a commission from the governor to
lead a local volunteer militia, Nathaniel Bacon decided to take
the protection of the frontier plantations into his own hands.
He answered the cries of "Bacon! Bacon! Bacon!" from over two
hundred western settlers who had encamped at Jordan's Point
near Bacon's landholdings. Bacon heard the call and led his "Volunteers," including Charles Clay, into Indian territory, where
they slaughtered Indians and commandeered supplies from the
settlers as they went.

Elizabeth Duke Bacon continues her account to her sister and
tells what happens next.

The Governour being very angry with him put out high things
against him, and told mee that he would most certainly hang him
as soon as hee returned, which hee would certainly have done; but
what for fear of the Governour's hanging him; and what for fear
of the Indians killing him brought mee to this sad condicion, but
blessed be God hee came in very well, with the losse of a very few
men; never was known such a fight in Virginia with so few men's
losse. The fight did continue nigh a night and a day without any
intermission. They did destroy a great many of the Indians, thanks
bee to God, and might have killed a great many more, but the Gov-
ernour were so much the Indians' friend and our enemy, that hee

sent the Indians word that Mr. Bacon was out against them, that
they might save themselves.

After Mr. Bacon was come in hee was forced to keep a guard of
soldiers about his house, for the Governour would certainly have
had his life taken away privately, if he would have had opportunity;
but the country does so really love him, that they would not leave
him alone any where; there was not any body against him but the
Governour and a few of his great men . . .

Elizabeth tells her sister how much Nathaniel is admired by
his men—"you never know any better beloved than hee is"—and
that the governor has sent his wife back to England "with great
complaints to the King against Mr. Bacon." Then she tells how
Nathaniel finally got his commission.

[The Indians] have murdered and destroyed a great many whole
families since, and the men resolving not to goe under any but your
brother, most of the country did rise in Armes, and went down to
the Governour, and would not stir till hee had given a commission
to your brother which hee has now done. He is made Generall of the
Virginia Warr, and now I live in great fear, that hee should loose his
life amongst them. They are come verry nigh our Plantation where
we live.

And there she ended. Elizabeth mailed her letter one month
before Bacon made his most rebellious move. On July 29, 1676,
with enough men to overpower Governor Berkeley's small force
in Jamestown, Nathaniel Bacon seized and torched Virginia's
first colony. Then Giles Bland, Bacon's friend and neighbor and
now head of the rebel's naval forces, chased Berkeley and his
navy down the James River toward the Bay. With Berkeley out

of the picture for the time being, Nathaniel Bacon decided to return to his alleged war plan to kill Indians. And this became his undoing.

While searching with his volunteers for Indians hiding in swamps invested with parasites, lice, and mosquitoes, Bacon contracted malaria. He was shaking with fever when he led his men out of the Great Dragon Swamp at summer's end. He was further weakened when he found that in the weeks he had been away from Jamestown, Giles Bland and the Rebellion's entire fleet of ships had been captured by Berkeley's forces.

Governor Berkeley did not get a chance to hang the rebel leader. Nathaniel Bacon died on October 26, 1676, of the "bloody flux" and "Lousey Disease." Several of Bacon's military command were tried and hanged—including Bland—in March of the next year along with twenty-two other volunteers. Governor Berkeley allowed the rest of the rebels—including Charles Clay, who had been recognized as he foraged livestock to feed the troops and was identified in court—to return to their land as long as they admitted their wrongdoing.

I tried to tell myself as I read Elizabeth's letter and learned more about the rebellion that Charles Clay thought he was doing his duty by joining a militia of frontiersmen under Bacon's leadership. In his mind—I told myself—he was protecting his family from future Indian attacks and securing the land rights of the Clay family. After all, I said to myself, Charles did not know what I knew about this moment in history. He did not know when he joined Bacon and the others at Jordan's Point—land adjacent to his father's first land patent—that the rebellion would turn bad. Nor did he know at the beginning of the rebellion that Bacon was not just interested in fighting the Indians but that he was gripped with a pathological desire to wrest power from the

Crown, crippled by a compelling need to drive Governor Berkeley—to whom he was related by marriage—out of Jamestown.

As I continued to research Bacon's Rebellion I learned that as the rebellion—or "revolution," as some recent scholars refer to it—grew in numbers, many landowners were forced by threats against their homes and families to forage food for the swelling number of settlers who had fallen under Nathaniel Bacon's charismatic spell. Perhaps Charles was not involved with Bacon on his own accord.

There is no way to know the fine points of Charles's decision, and I lose sight of him after the Rebellion. I can no longer picture Charles, but I can picture Hannah. As I imagine it, there were uncomfortable moments between Charles and Hannah Clay that spring of 1677 when Charles returned to Westover Parish. I assume that Hannah supported her husband's choice to join the rebel militia when it meant protection for her family from the marauding Indians. I cannot believe, however, that she supported Charles's choice—if he did have a choice—to follow Nathaniel Bacon to Jamestown in order to overthrow the Crown. It comforts me to believe that at least one of my relatives might have had the sense to recognize that Bacon's overthrow of the governor's forces was pure megalomania, despite Elizabeth Duke Bacon's perceptions of her husband.

Charles died suddenly in late spring 1686—nine years after the Rebellion of 1676 ended. He was alive in April when he recorded a document in Henrico County Courts and then he was dead. He was only forty-one. On June 1, 1686, Hannah distributed gifts to her children from their father's estate:

I give to John Clay, Thomas Clay, Henry Clay, and Charles Clay, my sons, each 1 cow 4 years old with calf by her side, at attaining age, also 1 well-fixed gun. To my daughter Judith Clay, 6 new pewter plates at her marriage or when of age.

I can still see Hannah and I grieve with her. She is forty-four. She has five under-age children. To make it worse, her father, John Wilson Senior, had died less than eighteen months before Charles's untimely death. She was not prepared to grieve again so soon.

Hannah inherited property on Swift Creek from her father's estate, yet she continued to live in Westover Parish. Sometime before October 1, 1687, Hannah married Edward Stanley—a marriage that lasted for the next twenty years. Hannah Wilson Clay Stanley died in the summer of 1706. On August 20, 1706, Edward Stanley was ordered "to bring the remaining orphans of Charles Clay to the next Court to discharge the securities of their estates." Although I cannot be certain, I think it is then that Henry Clay, Charles and Hannah's fifth child and third son, inherited his mother's property on Swift Creek. Whenever it was, Henry Clay, my great-great-great great-great-great-grandfather, made his home near the second falls of Swift Creek and was buried at the family plantation on Swift Creek called The Raells.

3

FAMILY REUNION

ENRY AND Mary Mitchell Clay's plantation, The Raells, was the setting for one of the most intriguing and frightening stories I was told when I was young. Before I tell the story, however, I will slip back into my Southern roots and classify Henry in his proper slot in the bloodline.

The "first Henry Clay," as the family often referred to him, was born in 1672, the son of Charles and Hannah Wilson Clay and the grandson of John Thomas and Elizabeth Claye. More important to the family than Henry's pedigree, however, were the sons he sired and the offspring who followed. Henry had four sons: William Mitchell, Henry, Charles, and John. He was the grandfather of Green Clay—the largest land and slaveholder in what became Kentucky. He was the great-grandfather of Henry Clay—statesman and presidential candidate—and of Cassius Marcellus Clay—abolitionist advisor to President Lincoln and ambassador to Russia. He was also the grandfather of my great-

great-great-great-great-great-grandfather, Mitchell Clay—"our
Revolutionary War soldier."

Henry was fourteen when his father, Charles, suddenly died
and thirty-four when he was finally orphaned by Hannah's death.
Little was known about him during that period beyond the
records of his inheritances from each parent and his various land
purchases. Then, around 1708 or 1709, Henry, age thirty-six or
thirty-seven, married Mary Mitchell, age fifteen or sixteen. The
Mitchells, like the Clays, were early colonizers. Mary's parents,
William and Elizabeth Innes Mitchell, owned land on Swift
Creek next to one of the Clay properties, making the liaison
between Mary and Henry expected and effortless.

Henry Clay supported his family well as a planter, trader, surveyor, land speculator, and appraiser. By the time of his death he
owned enough land—including the patents he inherited from
his father and grandfather—to leave each of his four sons two
plantations and several slaves. His will, written on March 28,
1749, tells the story.

In the name of God this Twenty eighth day of March in the year
of our lord Christ one thousand seven hundred & forty nine I
Henry Clay of Henrico County being of perfect health mind
memory thanks be to God therefore, and calling to mind my
mortality, and knowing that it is appointed for all men once to
die, do make and ordain this my last will and Testament that is
to say princably and first of all I give my Soul into the hands of
God that gave it, and as for my body I commend it to the earth,
to be buried in a Christian like and decent form at the discretion
of my Executors, nothing doubting but at the general resurrec-
tion I shall receive the same again by mighty power of God; and
as touching my worldly estate wherewith it hath pleasest God

to bless me in this life I give devise and dispose of the same in manner and form—

Imprimis I give and bequeath unto my Son William Clay the land and plantation whereon he now lives and my land and plantation on Deep Creek in Henrico County whereon Richard Belcher now lives to him and his heirs and assigns forever.

Item. I give and bequeath unto my son Henry Clay the land and plantation whereon he now lives and two hundred acres of land at Letalone in Goochland County it being the lower survey belonging to me at the same Letalone to him and his heirs forever and assigns.

Item. I give and bequeath unto my son Charles Clay the plantation whereon he now lives and all the land on the north side of Swift Creek and upper side of Nuttree Run to me belonging and also four hundred acres at Letalone being my upper survey at Letalone to him and to his heirs forever and assigns.

Item. I give and bequeath unto my son John Clay the plantation whereon he now lives and all my land on the north side of Swift Creek and upper side of Nuttree Run to him and to his heirs forever and assigns.

Item. I likewise give and bequeath my grist mill on Nuttree Run to be equally divided between my son Charles and my son John Clay to be held in Joint tenancy to them and to their heirs and assigns forever.

Item. I give to my daughter Amey Williamson five pounds current money.

Item. I give to my daughter Mary Watkins five pounds current money.

Item. I give and bequeath unto my grandson Henry Clay two hundred and forty acres of land adjoining to James Hill to him and his heirs and assigns forever.

Item. I give and bequeath unto my granddaughter Mary Clay daughter of Charles Clay one negroe girl named Phebe to her and her heirs and assigns forever.

Item. I give unto Mary, my well beloved wife, the plantation whereon I now live during her natural life and my negroe man Lewis, also my negroe Joe, and Sue and Hannah and Jenny, and Sarah during her natural life and what stock and household goods she pleases to have or make use of, of mine.

Item. I devise that the rest of my slaves not heretofore given and stock and household goods be given and equally divided among my four sons aforementioned at their discretion and also the negroes above written and gave to my wife may be equally divided after my wifes decease and the stock and household goods to her given also be divided all in manner and form afore-mentioned to my four sons above written and to their heirs and assigns forever.

Item. I give to my four sons aforesaid and to my wife to be equally divided all the ready money and money out at use that I shall be possessed with at my death.

Item. After my wifes decease, I give my plantation whereon I now live to my son John and to his heirs and assigns forever together with the adjacent land therein belonging and I do hereby make constitute and ordain my four sons above written to be my only and sole executors of this my last will and Testament declaring all former wills by me to be void and vocated of no effect declaring this and no other to be my last will and Testament. In Witness whereof I have hereunto sett my hand and affixed my seal the day and year above written.

Signed sealed and acknowledged before us Henry Clay.

The Raells, "the plantation whereon I now live," sat on Swift Creek a few miles south of present-day Richmond. It is there that Henry's chief story takes place. It concerns his death. Henry's headstone sets up the action. The inscription reads: *In memory of Henry Clay who died at dinner with his children and grandchildren at the annual festival given them in 1760.* The family storytellers, however, added two bits of information to the gravestone summary, two additions that transformed a potentially uninspiring story into high drama: Henry died of "the nattles" and he died face down in his dinner plate. In my young imagination I could see—and hear—it all. I still can.

I can see Henry and Mary's four sons and two daughters plus the adult grandchildren and all the spouses lined up and down a long table made of wide boards set on rough wood trestles. The family is eating outside under the golden parasol branches of a giant chestnut tree. Mary is not sitting at the foot of the table as she usually does at these family gatherings; rather she is sitting beside Henry at the head of the table because this is a special reunion. It marks Henry's birthday. The adults are talking loudly, voices pitched to be heard over the countless conversations that lace back and forth and up and down the length of the table. The younger cousins are playing tag and hide-and-seek among the trees, and the older boys have found a coil of heavy rope in the barn to start a tug of war. The sounds are happy, full, saturated with tonal color.

And then there is silence. Not full silence at first, but a creeping silence that starts at the head of the table where Henry had presided a moment ago. The silence floats toward the table's foot, stilling one conversation and then the next, until the daughters and the sons sitting at the far end of that long family table realize that all talk has stopped but theirs, and the silence becomes complete. When Mary gasps, and the sons and grandsons leap to Henry's side, the young cousins sense something terrible has happened and their play-filled laughter stops. That is what I saw and heard when the manner of Henry Clay's death was described.

That story made an impact on me. Henry's strange and sudden death freed my imagination to roam among my envisioned relatives while they ate and played under the trees at the family plantation, but there was more. It also frightened me. I think I was scared because no one could tell me what "the nattles" was. As a child I worried. What if I got "the nattles" and died at the dinner table? What if I could not get my breath and everyone around me was talking to someone and no one noticed? What if I died with my face down in a plate?

Henry's death story was the high point of the family narration about the third generation of our "ancient planter" ancestors. There was, however, another story about Henry and Mary Clay that was not passed down through the family. I uncovered it in the record of a court document at the Newberry Library. In 1712 it seems that Henry Clay kidnapped three Choctaw children in the Carolinas and brought them back to Swift Creek as slaves.

Here's what I could piece together. During his twenties and thirties, Henry, like his father, Charles, traded with the Indians for furs. In September 1712 Henry arrived back on Swift Creek after an eighteen-month trip in the Carolinas. He was not alone. With him were three Indian children. He sold one of the children and kept two—a girl he named Chance and a boy he called James. Sixty years later—in April 1772—the grandchildren of

Chance and James sued several of Henry and Mary Clay's grandchildren for their freedom on the grounds that their grandparents had been kidnapped.

The court sent an officer to depose Mary.

Mary Clay, aged eighty five, relict of Henry Clay, Deceased, being first duly sworn on the wholly Evangelists of Almighty God deposeth and saith

that she remembers her Husband, Henry Clay, brought in three Indians, two he kept, a boy & a girl. She was named Chance by the said Clay. And this Deponent further saith

that she believes that Ned, Peter, Sam & Rachell, Plaintiffs, are the descendents of the Indian Girl Chance which was brought in by the said Henry Clay. And further this deponent saith

that her husband, Henry Clay, told her he bought five Indians and a Negro which Negro dyed on the way and two of the Indians. And this deponent further saith

that her husband bought the said Indians, as she understood, of a white man and it was as far beyond Carolina as it was to it and that the Indians that he, her husband, brought in were Choctaws and that he carried horses and labored himself, as she was informed by her husband, and bought the said Indians in that way and that he gave eighteen pounds for one and twenty one for the other, as he the said Clay told this deponent, and that he was gone eighteen months from home, and further saith not.

John Clay, Henry's grandson and the father of the "other" Henry Clay, confirmed what his grandmother had said. He had asked his grandfather in 1756 or 1757 what nation of Indians Chance and James came from. Henry told him that they were

Chickasaws or Choctaws—John couldn't remember which—and that Henry said he had bought them from other Indians. He also testified that

> he heard said Henry Clay say he was obliged to come in very privately being in much danger as well of Indians as white people, and that he was obliged to cross the, Deponent believes, Roanoke River in a piece of bark headed with Deerskins.

Unfortunately for the Clay family, there was other testimony that did not corroborate that of wife and grandson. First was that of Matthew Farley of Powhatan County. Matthew was an old acquaintance of the Clay boys and had been a neighbor of Henry's brother Charles. Matthew Farley swore that Henry had frequently told him that when he traded to the Indian nation he had seen the children playing a short distance outside the Indian village he had just left. He grabbed up two of them and rode two days without stopping in case he was followed.

And then Elizabeth Blankinship, aged eighty-five and connected to the Clay family through her husband, who had been Henry Clay's stepbrother, told her story.

> Henry Clay, now deceased, told [her] that he took these Indians, to wit a Boy and a Girl, from their own Nation unbeknown to their friends & relations and, nigh as [she] remembers, he, the said Clay, told her that he hid underground for about a fortnight for fear the Indians should take away his Indians and knock him in the head.

On May 4, 1773, a General Court jury in North Carolina—where the branch of the Clay family that now owned the two

Indians lived—found for the plaintiffs. The grandchildren of Chance and James—Ned, Lucy, Silvia, Bristol, Chance, Frank, Peter, Sam, and Rachell and her children—were found "free and not slaves." The Clay family was penalized five pounds and charged with the court costs.

Mary Mitchell Clay died in August 1777 of the "flux," five years after the trial and the humiliating gossip about the Clays in both Virginia and North Carolina. It is likely that she was buried next to her husband in the small family graveyard at the The Raells, but only Henry's grave was marked.

This story about a significant Clay family trial did not get passed down as had other major family events such as John Thomas's marriage to Ann Nichols or Charles Clay's participation in Bacon's Rebellion. The kidnapping—and the resulting conflicting depositions that may have constituted outright perjury on Mary Clay's part and that of her grandson—was either easily forgotten or intentionally edited out of the Clay saga. After I found the records of the trial I began to wonder what other stories had been left out. What other stories had been forgotten? What other stories perhaps did not fit the family image the storytellers wanted us children to carry forward? Before long in my research I came across another untold tale—this one about Mitchell Clay and his wife, Phoebe Belcher, both grandchildren of Henry and Mary Clay. But before I relate it I have to set the stage by moving two generations of the family toward Virginia's western frontier, where the story takes place.

4

MYSTERIES

WILLIAM MITCHELL Clay, as the family called him—or William Clay, as he called himself—had four stories that flowed down the river of our family's oral history. Three were about key episodes in his life: birth, marriage, and death. The fourth was about his three brothers. None of them—except for the names of his brothers and their offspring—turns out to be clear-cut. I did not realize when I started on this historical detective venture what a muddle of facts and misinformation I would have to disentangle regarding my great-great-great-great-great-grandfather.

William Mitchell Clay was born sometime around 1710 and named for his maternal grandfather, William Mitchell. There were hushed speculations—based on the inclusion of "Mitchell" in the baby's name—that William Mitchell Clay was born out of wedlock. Yet, because the Henrico County, Virginia, marriage records for 1708–09 were lost during the burning of Richmond during the Civil War, the family found it easy to shrug off the matter. It would have been such an unfortunate precedent for the Clay girl-children, who were repeatedly and emphatically informed that "no one in our family has ever had a baby out of wedlock." Despite the possible illegitimacy, there was never a question in the family's mind that William Mitchell was indeed Henry and Mary Clay's child. Henry's will bore out the bloodline of his oldest child.

Whatever his actual birth date, William Mitchell Clay grew up in the arms of a large, well-established extended family. Both the Mitchells and the Clays owned plantations up and down Swift Creek starting in Henrico County—later Chesterfield County—between present-day Richmond and Petersburg and moving west along the rivers into the newly partitioned counties of Cumberland, Powhatan, and Goochland. Uncles, aunts, and cousins on both sides lived in close proximity, witnessed court documents for each other, and served as executors of estates. Further, they shared in family celebrations like Henry and Mary Mitchell's annual late-summer gatherings. From childhood on I have pictured William Mitchell as the first to jump up when his father's face fell forward into his plate at his last fateful birthday celebration.

According to the family, William Mitchell Clay married Ann Lewis around 1733. Interestingly, in all my memories of hearing Ann Lewis's name, she was never spoken of by her name alone. Instead she was consistently referred to as "Ann Lewis, the sister of General Andrew Lewis." Ann and Andrew were the children of Scots-Irish parents, John Lewis and Margaret Lynn, who lived on an estate in County Donegal that John managed until the couple was forced to flee Ireland over a dispute with their English landlord. Around 1726 John, Margaret, their four—or possibly five—children, including Andrew, and thirty-one of their tenant farmers sailed to Virginia.

The family settled in Augusta County, at the head of the Shenandoah Valley on Virginia's western frontier, and started over. John Lewis soon made a name for himself as a surveyor and—as did most surveyors of the period—claimed prime parcels of land for himself. Andrew, who worked with his father and George Washington, also made large claims on choice land. Andrew Lewis's landholdings were not, however, what brought his name to the lips of the Clay mothers as they told the family's history to their children. Andrew's fame came from his prowess in war—from his roles in the ongoing battles in the Indian Wars and from his participation in the Revolutionary War.

The stories of Andrew and John Lewis's surveying trips and Andrew's military exploits are well documented and do have a connection to William Mitchell Clay's later life. The premise that Revolutionary War hero Andrew Lewis was a relative of ours, however, turns out to be false. After days of researching several Lewis family lines and trying to mesh Ann Lewis into the family story as I knew it, I realized that the dates simply did not work. "Ann Lewis, the sister of General Andrew Lewis," was not born until 1728—two years after the family arrived in Virginia—and, consequently, could not have mothered William Mitchell's first child, William Clay, born in 1735.

Numerous Clay family historians have tried to make the Ann Lewis story fit. Some say that the Ann Lewis William Mitchell married was not the daughter of John and Margaret Lewis; rather, she was the daughter of another John Lewis and his wife Elizabeth Warner of Warner Hall in Gloucester County, Virginia. I followed the lead.

The daughter of John and Elizabeth Lewis was born in 1712 and would have been an appropriate age to marry and give birth to Baby William Clay in 1735. Yet examination of marriage records from the seventeenth and early eighteenth centuries indicated that the Clays and other early colonist families usually married within their neighboring geographic regions. Gloucester County, located on a peninsula formed by the Chesapeake Bay on the east and the York River on the west, is both distant from the Clay's and Mitchell's plantations and separate from the transportation network traveled by them: the James River, the Appomattox River, and Swift Creek. By now in my research surrounding the development of the early colonies—both north and south—I had learned the power of the rivers. I could feel the flow of the currents, the depth and the swerve of the channel on the James and its tributaries. "Ann Lewis from Gloucester County" came from the region of the York River and the Bay. She did not fit into the marriage patterns of the time.

I continued my search through historical documents—now somewhat obsessively—looking for my great-great-great-great-great-grandmother. Finally I found Martha Runyon. Martha was born about 1713 in Henrico County and died in January 1764 in Cumberland County. Little is known about her background, yet she fits the marriage pattern. She was a Henrico County neighbor of William Mitchell Clay, and she moved west with him as he bought and sold land. Further, hers is the only name of a spouse linked with William Mitchell in a land indenture, this one filed on January 21, 1764, in Cumberland County when William and Martha Clay sold land to Mathew Moseley.

Still, oral tradition does not die easily. Ann Lewis's story in the family history was so strong that some Clay family researchers melded Ann Lewis's name with the Cumberland County court document. For this group of family historians, William Mitchell's wife was Martha Ann Lewis, another daughter of John and Elizabeth Lewis in Gloucester County—once again a choice that does not work because of lack of proximity.

The story of William Mitchell Clay's wives does not end there. In my research I discovered that some Clay genealogists mentioned Agnes as his wife—actually as one of his wives. This group of family historians tended to cut their losses by listing all three women—Ann Lewis, Martha, and Agnes—as consecutive wives of William Mitchell. There was a source for Agnes. On September 22, 1768, a box ad appeared in the *Virginia Gazette*—a weekly publication circulated out of Williamsburg. The ad was paid for by William Clay of Cumberland County.

Cumberland, Sept. 8, 1768

Whereas my wife Agnes has eloped from my bed, and robbed me of things of considerable value, and I expect will endeavour to run me in debt, I therefore forewarn all persons from dealing with her on my account, as I will pay no debts of her contracting.

William Clay

I was excited to hold a copy of this paper in my hands and read the happenings of the week in the colony. Yet by then I had enough firm dates for William Mitchell to know that this William Clay could not be our William Clay. By September 1768 William Mitchell was living in Bedford County on the eastern slopes of the Blue Ridge Mountains near present-day Roanoke. He had joined several of his children there and already begun to purchase and sell land.

So, is my great-great-great-great-great-grandmother Martha Runyan? Martha is the only potential wife who grew up in Clay territory. Further, her dates are correct to have married William Mitchell and to have mothered his first child, William, born in 1735. Finally, Martha is credibly linked to William Clay in a land indenture. Sadly—as with the wedding date of William Mitchell

Clay's parents—the truth can never be verified. All Henrico County records of marriages between 1680 and 1784—the time and place where William Mitchell would have married—also were destroyed by fire.

As with his marriages, William Mitchell Clay has more than one death story. Each, interestingly, is connected to General Andrew Lewis. The family historians who so persistently kept "Ann Lewis, the sister of General Andrew Lewis," in the family tree—like my grandmother and her grandmother—may have fallen prey to one of the hazards of oral history. Much like the rumor that gets whispered around a circle ends up in laughable confusion between start and end, the stories of William Mitchell's marriage and death may have merged over generations of telling. The death story I was told places William Mitchell at the Battle of Point Pleasant on October 10, 1774—part of "Dunmore's War" against the Indians. The story unfolds in the following way.

In August 1774 Lord Dunmore, Governor of Virginia, directed Colonel Andrew Lewis, commander of the southwestern Virginia militia, to muster a volunteer army for a major attack against the Shawnee, Mingo, and Delaware tribes who lived along the Ohio River. Andrew Lewis, who had commanded regular army troops under George Washington in the French and Indian War, was given two months to raise a militia of eleven hundred men from Virginia's southwestern counties. He was directed to march them from Fort Union on the Greenbrier River in what became southeast West Virginia, down to the New River, where Virginia's border now meets West Virginia, north along the New, which turned into the Great Kanawha River, past present-day Charleston, West Virginia, and on to the mouth of the Kanawha on the Ohio River. Dunmore would lead his fifteen hundred regular army troops in a flotilla down the Ohio from Fort Pitt to join Colonel Lewis on October 1 at Point Pleasant—a triangular peninsula at the confluence of the Ohio and Kanawha rivers. Together, according to Lord Dunmore, they would sweep across Indian Territory in what would soon be known as Ohio.

Andrew Lewis's younger brother Colonel Charles Lewis was assigned to lead one group of the volunteer army and Colonel William Fleming another. Two of Andrew's sons had volunteered to fight with their father and uncle as privates. William Mitchell Clay, age sixty-four, had also volunteered as had—I discovered in my research of muster and pension records—three of his sons: Mitchell, Ezekiel, and David.

Andrew Lewis and his troops arrived at Point Pleasant on October 6, then waited for three days for Dunmore's army. Messengers scurried back and forth between the volunteer militia and the regular army telling of Dunmore's changing plans: he was still at Fort Pitt; he would come overland instead of by water. On October 9 the order came for Lewis to break camp, cross the Ohio, and march toward the Indian encampments, where Dunmore would meet him. The last three hundred of Lewis's Virginia troops were expected to arrive in a few hours. Andrew Lewis decided to start the Ohio crossing the next day. It was one day too late.

At dawn on Monday, October 10, 1774, the Indians—who had crept up to Lewis's camp during the night—attacked. The battle raged for hours with Lewis's troops backed against the two rivers. Finally, on news that more militia troops were moving up from the south, the Indians collected their dead and wounded and pulled back. Andrew Lewis lost seventy-five men—half of his commissioned officers, including his brother Charles, and fifty-two militiamen. According to the family story, William Mitchell Clay was one of the dead.

William Mitchell, however, has a possible second death story, which I found in Alexander S. Withers's *Chronicles of Border Warfare*, published in Virginia in 1831. In this account a volunteer named Clay died on September 10, 1764, while hunting deer for Colonel Field's volunteers on Little Meadows Creek on the way to the Battle of Point Pleasant:

> When the army was preparing to leave Camp Union, there was for a while some reluctance manifested on the part of Col. Field to submit to the command of Gen. Lewis. This proceeded from the fact, that in a former military service, he had been the senior of Gen. Lewis; and from the circumstances that the company led on by him were Independent Volunteers, not raised in pursuance of the orders of Governor Dunmore, but brought into the field by his own exertions, after his escape from the Indians at Kelly's. These circumstances induced him to separate his men from the main body of the army on its march, and to take a different way from the one pursued by it,—depending on his own knowledge of the country to lead them a practicable route to the river.
>
> While detached from the forces of Gen. Lewis, two of his men (Clay and Coward) who were out hunting and at some little distance from each other, came near to where two Indians were concealed. Seeing Clay only, and supposing him to be alone, one of them fired at him; and running up to scalp him as he fell, was himself shot by Coward.

According to Withers, Colonel Field, fearing an ambush, quickly advanced his forces to join Colonel Charles Lewis's troops, who had moved out in advance of both Colonel Field and his brother Andrew. A volunteer named Clay appears on the roster of Colonel Charles Lewis, with a note that he had been killed in September. As with William Mitchell Clay's birth and marriage stories, there is no way to determine the actual events of his death. All we know is that he died either in the Battle of Point Pleasant or on the way.

The single bit of information that the family chroniclers knew for certain about William Mitchell was that he had three brothers, and two of them were worth claiming as good story material. Interestingly, he also had two sisters, Mary Obedience and Amy, who were never mentioned. I discovered Mary Obedience in another context, which caused me to rethink what I had been told—or not told—about the family. But first the brothers.

Many southern families adorn their libraries with hand-drawn family trees. In a reverse photo process the roots, trunks, leafless branches, and twigs are black, and on each branch and twig is the name in white script of a parent and spouse and the children begat in the marriage. William Mitchell had three younger brothers—Henry, Charles, and John. It is here in this fourth generation of Clays in America that the various lines of the Clay family tree begin to divide. While John Thomas Claye followed by Charles Clay form leader roots for the Clay tree, Henry and Mary Mitchell form the trunk from which the family lines begin to branch off.

William Mitchell's brother Henry, born a year after William Mitchell, was never mentioned in the family. Charles, William Mitchell's second brother, however, was popular with the storytellers because he fathered Green Clay, named for his mother, Martha Green. Green was a surveyor and soldier who was granted, then purchased, huge tracts of land in Kentucky. By the time Kentucky gained separation from Virginia in 1792, Green Clay owned most of central Kentucky and was on his way to being one of the most powerful political forces and largest slaveholders in the state.

Green Clay had a second story line in the family. He was the father of Cassius Marcellus "Cash" Clay. Cassius Clay was born in October 1810 in the downstairs bedroom at White Hall, the family estate in Madison County, Kentucky. He died ninety-three years later in the same room and, if family lore is accurate, in the bed in which he was born.

Kentucky abounded with Cash Clay stories: his dark-eyed handsomeness, his towering height for the time of six feet three inches, his fights with his bowie knife, his famous brass cannon that held off intruders more than once, his love affair with a Russian ballerina and duel using the bowie knife with her aristocratic husband, his rushed escape from St. Petersburg with a nude portrait of his lover under his arm, the surprise arrival in Kentucky of his young Russian son and nanny during a family dinner party. These were Clay family stories. They were Kentucky stories.

Cassius Clay, however, had more substance than the commonwealth's favorite stories suggested. He was well educated—trained in the classics, oratory, and the law—and was elected numerous times to the Kentucky legislature. First and foremost, however, he was an abolitionist, having formed his views regarding slavery during his college years at Yale. Although when Green Clay died in 1827 seventeen-year-old Cassius inherited dozens of slaves, along with White Hall (then called Clermont) and twenty-two hundred acres of Madison County, he freed them when he reached his majority. Cassius spoke on issues of slavery throughout the northern states and once for his cousin when Henry Clay ran for president on the Whig ticket in 1844 against James K. Polk.

When Henry Clay lost his bid for president, Cassius returned to Kentucky with his own chances for continued political campaigns tarnished. In 1844 he started an abolitionist press—*True American*—in Lexington, Kentucky. Eventually the press was overrun by an angry mob of slaveholders, whom Cassius—though seriously wounded in the siege—held off with a cannon faced squarely at the door.

In 1860, when he was nearly fifty, Cassius Clay's picture was published in *Harper's Weekly* along with nine others who were considered potential presidents. Cassius, however, threw his support behind Abraham Lincoln and campaigned for him in both North and South. Following his election, Lincoln rewarded Cassius with the ambassadorship to Russia. Before Cassius left on his new assignment, however, Fort Sumter in South Carolina was attacked, and there was fear that Washington might also be attacked. According to contemporary accounts, Cassius calmly strolled through the White House halls with three pistols strapped to his chest and a bowie knife tied tightly to his leg while Lincoln huddled with advisors over next steps.

Cassius spent nearly a decade in Russia, returning to America briefly in 1862 at Lincoln's request to assess Kentucky's sentiment regarding the emancipation of slaves. After meeting with Kentucky leaders, Cassius returned to Washington with the conviction that Kentucky would remain neutral should Lincoln free southern slaves. He then sailed back to Russia.

My favorite Cassius Clay story happens late in his life, when he was in retirement in Kentucky, writing and reading and, some would say, making trouble in Madison County. The date was November 14, 1894. Cassius was eighty-four and had just married Dora Richardson, who was barely fifteen. The good folks in Richmond, the county seat of Madison County—built on land that had once been Clay property—were not happy. They felt it was their duty to rescue Dora.

I have known and cherished this story for as long as I can remember. Still, rather than describe the event the way it was told to me—as a stern admonition against unacceptable behavior "even if he was a Clay"—I will use the eyewitness account of the sheriff, Josiah Simmons, which I recently found:

Richmond, Kentucky, November 14, 1894

Judge John C. Chenault, Dear Judge,

I am reporting about the posse like you said I had to. Judge, we went out to White Hall but we didn't do no good. It was a mistake to go out there with only seven men. Judge, the general was awful mad. He got to cussin' and shootin', and we had to shoot back. The old general sure did object to bein' arrested. Don't let nobody tell you he didn't, and we had to shoot. I thought we hit him two or three times, but don't guess we did. He didn't act like it. We come out right good considerin'. I'm having some misery from two splinters of wood in my side. Dick Collier was hurt a little when his shirt tail and britches was shot off by a piece of horseshoe and nails that come out of that old cannon. Have you seen Jack? He wrenched his neck and shoulder when his horse throw'd him as we were gettin' away. Judge, I think you'll have to go to Frankfort and see [Governor John Young] Brown. If he could send Captain Longmire up here with two light fielders, he could divide his men, send some with the cannon around to the front of the house, not too close, and the others around through the corn field and up around the cabins and spring house to the back porch, I think this might do it.

Respectfully, Josiah P. Simmons, High sheriff

I was fortunate to find another eyewitness account of the drama over Dora, this one from a man in his eighties whom I met in the early 1970s when I was in my early thirties and teaching at Berea College. He had been a young boy when the posse went to White Hall and had begged his father, Cassius's personal physician and part of the posse, to let him go along. His father finally agreed, he said, but only if he would stay way back and hide behind a tree. "You never knew what Ole Cash would do." So he watched while the posse approached and Cassius pulled his highly polished brass cannon out onto the second-floor balcony. He listened while the posse demanded Dora's return and Cassius yelled his invectives. And he ran when the posse turned tail with the cannon spewing nails and metal shards and broken horseshoes. He chuckled when he relived those exciting moments and repeated, "You never knew what Ole Cash would do." I relived the story with him.

Shortly before I met this man who'd seen "Ole Cash" in action, Mother and I had broken into derelict White Hall. We found a window that we could barely squeeze through and tiptoed from room to room in what Mother called "one of our family's homes." It is a time I will never forget.

The first floor was littered with tin cans and old blankets, cigarette butts and beer bottles. A charred area blackened the center of the once-fine inlaid floor—a place to warm the cans of soup whose remains were strewn about. We walked up the central stairs to the second floor and looked out across the front lawn—the lawn that the posse's horses had trotted across as they came to get Dora. Then I turned around and saw something that gave my family's history form.

The setting sun was streaming low through tilting half-closed shutters. Light spilled into the room and across the floor in stripes of ochre that glistened like gold dust on the motes stirred up by our footsteps. For a moment—a moment that I wanted to last and last—I lived at White Hall. I was at the parties my grandmother's grandmother had described. I heard the babble of cousins talking, the raucous banter of political exchange, the music from the dancing below. I saw my tall, handsome cousin with the dark eyes and shock of dark hair stride into a room. I saw him nod coolly toward his cousin Henry Clay and knew I was picturing an exchange after the presidential campaign, after the notorious dinner party where Cousin Henry stood up and blamed Cousin Cassius and his abolitionist views for his loss of the presidency to Polk back in 1844. I saw and felt it all—and I knew for that one instant what it felt like to accept that I was a Clay.

But it didn't last. I still had to deal with Henry Clay, the grandson of John Clay, William Mitchell's third brother. Henry's views on slavery angered and embarrassed me. I can still remember standing in my bedroom during one visit home from college. It was 1958, and I was already "sitting in" with black friends at lunch counters, movie houses, and churches. Mother and I were talking about the family, and she said with disgust, "I will never understand why you relate to that horrible man Cassius Clay when you have such a good example to follow in Henry Clay!" "Mother," I responded, "Henry Clay was not known as 'The Great Compromiser' for no reason."

Henry Clay was born on April 12, 1777, in Hanover County, Virginia. When he was four, his father, John, grandson of the first Henry Clay and a Baptist preacher and farmer, died. He received little formal education, but at age fifteen, while working as a deputy clerk in Virginia's High Court of Chancery, Henry was spotted by Chancellor George Wythe, who directed his studies in the classics and in oratory. After studying law with Robert Brooke, the former governor of Virginia, Henry passed the bar exam. It was 1799. Henry was only twenty, tall and lean. That year he made a propitious decision. Rather than stay in Virginia and be one of the many bright young lawyers from old families, he decided to make a career in what was then called the west.

In November 1787 Henry Clay moved to Lexington, Kentucky, and began to practice law, to disentangle land boundary lines claims from overlapping surveys, and to dip his toe in politics. Seventeen months later he married Lucretia Hart from a prominent Lexington family and began his active political career. For the rest of his life he served in either state or national government. Among other duties, he was sent to Ghent in 1814 by President James Madison to help negotiate the end of the War of 1812; he served as secretary of state under John Quincy Adams; he was speaker of the house for years and gained the sobriquet of one of the "Great Triumvirate" when he moved to the Senate along with two other master politicians, Daniel Webster and John Calhoun.

I tried to like Henry Clay, to be impressed by my famous relative. But I could not. He was a slaveholder, and there were rumors that he hired cruel overseers who beat the Clay slaves and split up slave families. But most of all I could not accept Henry's stand on slavery: his championship of gradual emancipation, his view that Congress had no right to impose laws on existing slave states, his proposal of the future colonization of slaves in Africa. It was Henry who, when questioned during the presidential campaign season in 1839 about his anti-abolitionist views, made the famous statement "I had rather be right than president" and then failed to win his expected nomination for the spot on the Whig ticket.

When my eighth-grade class made a field trip to Ashland, Henry and Lucretia Hart Clay's elegant home in Lexington— as all Kentucky schoolchildren did—I told no one what I knew about my great-great-grandmother Kizzie Clay's tales of family visits there: that the "whole house glowed with kerosene lamps," that "the family spilled out onto the wide verandas laughing and talking and drinking mulled wine."

William Mitchell, the "first" Henry Clay's son, who was my ancestor, did not have such famous offspring. Still, he too furthered the dream of his great-great-grandfather, John Thomas Claye. He acquired land. He and his children moved across Virginia to bigger patents, longer vistas, richer river bottoms. He fought in America's wars and fathered sons and daughters who would continue in his path. His son Mitchell Clay, my great-great-great-great-grandfather, was the first settler in what would become Mercer County, West Virginia. And Mitchell's son William Clay would move my branch of the family into eastern Kentucky.

5

FAMILY SECRETS

TWO TRAGEDIES I discovered when I began to research my family serve as a reminder that the oft-quoted saying "what goes around comes around" may well be true. I feel sure that it did not occur to those closest to the incidents to connect a sudden decision that Henry Clay made in 1712 with an event that happened at Clover Bottom in 1783. Yet in hindsight there is a distressing point-counterpoint in the sequence.

In the first case, Henry kidnapped three Indian children. In the second, Indians killed three of Henry's great-grandchildren. The massacre of the Clay children took place at their homestead on the Bluestone River in what is now Mercer County, West Virginia. The parents of the children killed were Mitchell and Phoebe Belcher Clay, my great-great-great-great-grandparents. As I have said earlier, the kidnapping story was never mentioned in the family. Inexplicably, the massacre of the children was referenced only in brief, even though it was so well known in Virginia and West Virginia in the late nineteenth century that it could be described in detail over a hundred years after it occurred.

Before I tell the story of the massacre, I need to place Phoebe and Mitchell on the family tree. I was in for a surprise when I delved into this fifth generation of Clays on Virginia's soil. Mitchell was the fourth child of William Mitchell Clay and Martha Runyon. Phoebe was the fourth child of Richard Belcher and Mary Obedience Clay, Mitchell's sister. Phoebe Belcher and Mitchell Clay were each grandchildren of Henry and Mary Mitchell Clay. Phoebe and Mitchell were first cousins.

When I moved to Ann Arbor—to the "North" as the family called it—I was teased about being from Kentucky. Frequent references were made regarding outhouses, shoes, and, of course, cousins marrying cousins. I would simply smile and say, "None of that in my family." I was wrong, but I did not know it until I began to research the family generation by generation. Phoebe Clay had always been referred to in my hearing as "Phoebe Belcher." No one ever mentioned that her mother was Mary Obedience Clay or that Henry and Mary Mitchell Clay—favorites in the recitation of the bloodline—were not just Mitchell's grandparents but Phoebe's grandparents as well. I am not sure my mother and grandmother knew. If they did, they never spoke of it. Nor was it mentioned that Elizabeth Clay, the first child of William Mitchell and Martha Runyon, married Isham Belcher, the first child of Richard and Mary Obedience Belcher—another first-cousin marriage.

Mitchell Clay was the family's designated Revolutionary War soldier—even though several men who married into the family also had fought for independence. I can remember clearly the angry tone of Mother's voice when she rebuked me for refusing to attend the meetings of the Daughters of the American Revolution: "You will be a member of DAR. I entered you on Mitchell Clay's name"—she had entered on Jerome Burns on her maternal great-grandfather's side—"and that is something to be proud of." It appears, however, that Mitchell Clay, our Revolutionary War designee, may have sat out the war.

In support of the family story line, Mitchell Clay's name does appear on a Revolutionary War document. The document, however, is not a muster record of actual engagement or a warrant book of land grants to those who served in the militia or regular army. Rather Mitchell Clay's name appears on a list of Revolutionary War Public Service Claims. In May 1780 Virginia's General Assembly authorized the governor to impress equipment and supplies for the Continental Army in each of Virginia's counties. Mitchell Clay provided supplies for Washington's troops. In exchange he was given a certificate of valuation. Starting in 1781 those who provided materiel could file a claim for reimbursement. Mitchell Clay filed his claim, and that seems to sum up his engagement in the Revolutionary War.

This discovery fit into the pinpoint research I was doing on the impact of the revolution on Virginia's western counties. Although there were frequent military actions in the northern states and some in the southern ports, the western regions of the mid-Atlantic had limited involvement.

My research in the Library of Virginia's extensive online document database turned up several references to Mitchell's involvement in Dunmore's War, including photocopies of his muster records. Yet his name only appears once—the claim for reimbursement for impressed supplies—in the Revolutionary War documents. The absence of his name in the militia records answered the questions I had been asking: Why did Mitchell Clay fight in the Revolutionary War when few from the mountain region did? How could he have settled the land on Clover Bottom where the massacre occurred and live there without incident between 1775 and 1783, as local historians reported, if he had fought in the war for a term of months or a year? The answer was simple. Mitchell Clay did not fight.

Interestingly, it was only when I became curious about the Belchers who married the Clays that I discovered the first-cousin marriages. And it was there—through the Belchers—that I began to piece together the Clay family's trek from the rich river bottoms and tobacco plantations on the James and Appomattox rivers to the hills and valleys of the Appalachian Mountains in Virginia's southwest territory. I began at this point in the saga to relate to my family, to relate because of the mountains I knew from the Kentucky side where our family eventually settled. Settled, that is, until I left. Also in that fifth generation of Clays in Virginia I started to recognize a family pattern, to see a repetition of life choices that I knew from my vantage point in the twenty-first century would continue for several more generations—and still more should my grandchildren decide to venture out beyond familiar territory.

In the 1760s and '70s the Clays and Belchers sought land, just as John Thomas Claye had done when he came to Jamestown in 1613, just as his grandson Henry Clay had done when he bought plantation after plantation along the Virginia waterways. And now it was Henry's grandchildren Mitchell and Mary Obedience Clay and Phoebe and Isham Belcher's turn to add land to the family holdings. But they were not alone. Other great-great-grandchildren of first colonizers were moving across Virginia toward the mountains in the southwest—including the Cecils, who in the next generation would marry into the Clay family and change our story line forever.

There was a parallel in this mid-eighteenth-century land quest to the one that had occurred one hundred fifty years before. Just as the Virginia Company offered land to adventurers who agreed to settle and work it, the English Crown once again made land available for settlement. This time the land was offered at limited cost so England could fill in the spaces of the territory that it claimed in order to show the French, the Spanish, and the Indians that this land belonged to England, that it belonged to the English-Americans who held the land grants.

Books on history tend to hit the high points of a culture or society. In the eyes of historians who make the decisions about those "defining moments," wars, plagues, droughts, starving times, and other periods of drama provide a lattice of reference points that they hope will characterize the times for their readers. Oral tradition reflects the same pattern. I knew John Thomas Clayc fought starvation and Indians along the James River. I knew Charles Clay fought in Bacon's Rebellion. I knew Henry Clay kept pushing the edges of the frontier both in his land purchases and in his trading and surveying, and that William Mitchell Clay died in Dunmore's War. I also had been told that Mitchell Clay fought in the Revolutionary War and lost children to the Indians. What no one talked about were the quiet moments in between. When I tried to get to know my great-great-great-great-grandparents Mitchell and Phoebe Belcher Clay, I discovered a decade of comparative quiet in the early history of the country and in the family.

The 1760s and early '70s were a less strident time, a comparatively safe time in Virginia, at least less strident and safer than it had been for years. In the northern colonies, Britain's ongoing battles with the French and Indians ended with the signing of the Treaty of Paris in 1763. In the southern colonies, the Cherokee,

Choctaw, and Chickasaw agreed to end the ever-increasing conflicts with the British over boundaries and trade. In 1763 a Proclamation Line was drawn along the ridge of the Allegheny Mountains. All lands draining to the west belonged to the Indians; those draining to the east were open to peaceful settlement. Before the drawing of the Proclamation Line of 1763, the Crown had encouraged Virginians to move toward the mountains, to fill in the spaces, and after, to spill over into Indian Territory on land grants held out from the agreement with the Indians, grants issued to those who fought in the French and Indian War.

Even before the end of the French and Indian War and the decade or so of relative peace with the Indian tribes in the south, the Clays went on the move. Around 1760, my branch of the Clay family decided to leave the bottomlands along the rivers of their forefathers. There are no diaries or letters that tell why, only deed books that cite land sales in Henrico and Chesterfield counties and land purchases in Bedford County. Then—as Bedford was divided again and again to make easier access to county seats for the recording of deeds and wills—the Clays and the Belchers filed claims in Franklin, Giles, and Tazewell counties.

Perhaps my part of the family left the plantations because tobacco had leached the rich river soil of nutrients. Tobacco did that. Perhaps it was because tobacco prices fell by 75 percent after 1760. Or perhaps there were no longer enough plantations in the family to be doled out. William Mitchell had inherited two plantations from his father, Henry, but William Mitchell had four sons of his own. Whatever the reason, the younger Clays and Belchers left their family homes and headed west. Mitchell Clay, around twenty, joined his older sister Elizabeth Clay and her husband, Isham Belcher, on the journey. Isham's sister Phoebe Belcher went along, as did Richard Bailey, who married Isham and Phoebe's sister Elizabeth Anne Belcher around this time. Together the kinship group—as anthropologists would refer to them—moved across Virginia.

I have read enough family accounts from this period to be able to imagine the young Clays and Belchers and Richard Bailey as they travel. I think that at first they considered going across Virginia on the rivers since river transportation was what they knew. But both the James and the Appomattox run northwest before they turn toward the south. So I imagine they decided to join other groups of fifth-generation Virginians—and the more recent Scots-Irish immigrants—and they walked beside their wagons and their packhorses toward the mountainous frontier.

As I picture my family group there is at least one bedstead tied to a thick-flanked horse with head and footboards framing a sharp roof peak over the horse's back. The heavy ropes that usually support the mattress ticking hold the bed rails in place along the horse's sides. The rails extend out slightly in front and behind, giving the sturdy animal a momentary long, lean look.

The bedstead is not the only thing that sets the family group apart. There are black slaves in the group. Few of the travelers heading to the mountains owned slaves, nor did they purchase them later. The Clays of this generation, however, had only known households and plantations that were supported by slaves passed from father to son in wills: from Henry Clay to his sons, from William Mitchell to his sons, from Mitchell to his sons. I am not sure how many black slaves were with them on the journey. All I know is that in 1774 Mitchell traded a "negro woman and her children" to John Draper for 803 acres of land—part of a land grant given to Draper for his role in the French and Indian War—and in his will written on July 26, 1810, and March 1811, Mitchell left at least one slave to each of his four sons.

Besides the bed and the slaves, "the children," as I imagine their parents still called them, have bags of cornmeal and some hog jowl, a couple of iron skillets and a large stew pot plus some pewter plates passed down from Clay mother to Clay daughter. The young couples gather around the family fire at night, tired but excited about their adventure. They tell each other that their trek toward new land investments is easy compared to the stories they have been told about John Thomas Claye—great-great-grandfather to both the Belchers and the Clays.

At first the Clays and the Belchers and Richard Bailey purchased land in Bedford County, southeast of present-day Roanoke—along what is now the Blue Ridge Parkway in Franklin County. Mitchell Clay married his cousin Phoebe Belcher in Bedford in April 1760—the same year their mutual grandfather Henry died at the August family reunion. Then in 1765 Mitchell's father, William Mitchell Clay, joined his children and nieces and nephew—presumably soon after his wife and the Clay children's mother, Martha Runyon, died. The extended family bought and sold land, and then bought some more.

By April 25, 1774, when "Notable Tracts of Land" were surveyed and listed by John Floyd, Hancock Taylor, and James Douglas, Mitchell and Phoebe owned "1000 acres both sides of Bluestone Cr., Clover Bottom" in Fincastle County, Virginia. In the fall of 1774 Mitchell Clay and his brothers David and Ezekiel joined John Robertson's Company for fifty-one days to fight in Dunmore's War. By 1775—after Mitchell had fought in the Battle of Point Pleasant, and after his father William Mitchell had been killed in the campaign—Mitchell and Phoebe were living on their land.

As was usual with kinship groups, the Clays and the Belchers and the Baileys spread out along the same river valley—in this

case along the Bluestone and the New River. Although the
family often lived on parcels five to ten miles apart, Mitchell
and Phoebe Belcher Clay felt safe. Even though they were in
Indian Territory, they were off the trails used by warriors to
move between hunting grounds. They had a large house for their
large family. They had fields of corn and grains and patches of
tobacco. They had an orchard. They had large pastures for their
cattle. Life was peaceful. Then it changed. In 1783—eight peaceful years after their move to Clover Bottom—Indians attacked
the family.

I knew little about this attack before I began my research. In
fact, Mitchell and Phoebe Belcher Clay's generation was summed
up in a brief narration that was always told in the same way. It
was the version that had been passed down to my grandmother,
through her mother, who had been told the story by her grandmother, who had married William Clay—who was born at Clover
Bottom and witnessed the attack. This version held that in 1774
Mitchell Clay, our Revolutionary War soldier, purchased a land
warrant from Lieutenant John Draper, who had been granted
the land for fighting in the French and Indian War. The warrant was for 803 acres on the Bluestone River at Clover Bottom,
where Mitchell and Phoebe Belcher lived until 1783 when Indians attacked and killed some of their children. After the attack
the family moved to a settlement on the New River where they
built a log house. Later a statue of Mitchell and Phoebe Belcher
Clay was erected in Princeton, West Virginia, the county seat of
Mercer County, to commemorate the Clay family as the first settlers of the county.

That was it. That was how the story was told each time. No
elaboration, just fact. That is not, however, the way Mitchell and
Phoebe's story was told to David E. Johnston for his book, *A*

History of the Middle New River Settlements and Contiguous Territory, published in 1906. In the late nineteenth century David Johnston traveled around the New River Valley gathering from the relatives of the early settlers stories that he corroborated with courthouse documents and trips to the sites of the original homesteads and settlements. As part of his research he stood next to the foundation stones of my great-great-great-great-grandparents' house on the rise above the Bluestone at Clover Bottom. In my imagination I have stood beside him and gazed across the landscape. Based on the various stories told to Johnston regarding the attack on Clover Bottom, this is what I see and hear.

It is late August 1783, and there is just the beginning of a rustle to the leaves in the first-growth forest that reaches down in chubby fingers behind the house. The large log house sits on a high spot in the rolling landscape of the wide Bluestone River valley. It is a big house, big enough for Phoebe and Mitchell Clay's fourteen children. The farmland that Mitchell and Phoebe and their children have so painstakingly nurtured tilts gently down to the riverbed. There are a thousand acres—all Mitchell and Phoebe's land with its rich bottomland fields of wheat and corn, its tobacco patches, the kitchen garden, Phoebe's orchard.

Phoebe stands by a small window watching Bartley and Ezekiel—her strapping teenage sons—build a fence to keep the cattle out of the grain they harvested with their father the day before. Mitchell got them started on the fence early, then set out hunting. In my mind I can see Phoebe gaze proudly at her boys there on the edge of the pasture. When the wind shifts our way we—Phoebe and I—can hear Bartley and Ezekiel's teasing banter over the steady rap-tap-tap of their hammers. Now we turn to look at Tabitha. Phoebe's teenage daughter is down by the river helping the younger girls wash. They are giggling and making rainbows with their soapy splashes.

Then, over the rustles, the laughter, the giggles and splashes, rings the sharp snap of a rifle shot. Phoebe moves quickly to the door. The younger girls are running toward the house crying, "Indians, Momma, Indians! They shot Bartley!" She looks toward the pasture. Bartley lies on the ground. Ezekiel struggles with several Indians who are holding him away from his brother. Tabitha is running toward Bartley. She grabs for the Indian's knife intended for her brother's scalp. Startled, he struggles with her, slashing her each time the knife changes hands.

Just then Liggon Blankenship, who has been hunting in the woods behind the house, comes to the back door. He hasn't seen the Indians. Phoebe pulls him to the front and begs him to shoot the Indian who is wrestling with Tabitha. "Save Tabitha! Save Tabitha!" Liggon Blankenship turns and runs back into the woods—a decision that becomes one of his stories and reflects on him and his family well beyond his death. Liggon runs toward the New River to tell the settlers that the Mitchell Clay family has just been slaughtered by Indians. Phoebe watches helplessly as Tabitha is slashed over and over until she dies sprawled across Bartley's body. Then in horror she sees the brother and sister scalped in turn.

The Indians drag Ezekiel away. Phoebe counts them in case she and the children can get help for Ezekiel. Eleven. There are eleven. With the help of the younger children she half carries, half drags Bartley and Tabitha's bodies into the cabin and lays them together on the bed. She has lost no children in childbirth. These are the first deaths. She must save the rest of her children. She must get them to John Bailey's blockhouse. The men in the river settlements must save Ezekiel. Phoebe makes the children, including my great-great-great-grandfather William, who is five, move as fast as they can through the six miles of woods to John Bailey's on the New River.

When Mitchell Clay returns from hunting that night he finds his two dead children on his and Phoebe's bed. Believing his entire family has been captured or killed, he leaves immediately for the settlements along the New River to put together a search party. At John Bailey's, Mitchell finds Phoebe and the children and learns of Ezekiel's capture. A party of eleven men led by Captain Matthew Farley—including John Bailey and Mitchell's young sons Charles and Mitchell Junior—leave immediately to pick up Ezekiel's trail. They stop at Clover Bottom on the way just long enough to bury Tabitha and Bartley.

The trail is easy to follow, and by evening of the day after the massacre the search party sees the smoke of the Indians' camp. The men hide in the woods until dawn, then open fire. Charles— age nine—wants desperately to avenge his brother and sister but the gun is too heavy for him to take good aim. Mitchell Junior ignores the pleas in broken English of a wounded Indian and shoots him in the chest. All of the Indians in the camp are slaughtered, but Ezekiel is no longer there. He has been taken ahead to Chillicothe, Ohio, where Mitchell and Phoebe later learn he was tortured and then burned at the stake.

Phoebe Belcher Clay sets a precedent for other Clay women. Phoebe refuses to return to the thousand acres on the Bluestone at Clover Bottom—the homestead where she and Mitchell raised their children, the big house that she loved so much. Phoebe and Mitchell move to the New River Valley, to Pearisburg, so Phoebe can be near her oldest daughter, Rebecca. Rebecca is married to Colonel George Pearis, who had founded the settlement the year before the attack. The Clays buy land and then more land. Mitchell builds Phoebe Belcher a house that—according to oral history—duplicates the one she lived in on Clover Bottom.

In the late 1890s, when David Johnston collected the data for his book, Mitchell and Phoebe's Pearisburg house still stood, and he photographed it. The hewn-log house is two stories tall with a peaked roof. Vertical slots in the upper level—narrow on the outer wall, widening toward the interior—allow for the noses and sights of rifles. Two large lower rooms are separated by a wide dog run. Windows open on the front from which Phoebe can see her daughter Rebecca's home directly across the road.

In September 1787—four years after the assault—my great-great great-great-grandparents sold half of their thousand acres at Clover Bottom to Hugh Innes. Three years later they conveyed the remaining half of the Clover Bottom tract to their son-in-law, George Pearis. With the land sales, the historic account of the massacre at Clover Bottom comes to an end.

Mitchell Clay died in 1811. Phoebe Belcher Clay died two years later, thirty years after the massacre of her children along the Bluestone River. She was still living in Pearisburg when she died. I like to think that her daughter, Rebecca Clay Pearis, was with her.

More than a century later, the citizens of Mercer County, West Virginia, erected the stone statue to mark the loss experienced by the first family to settle in the region. Phoebe holds a baby, and Mitchell Clay stands tall and tight against her. Grief shows hard and cruel on their faces, and I imagine that local residents sometimes hear wails over the whispers of the wind in the evening, the wind that sometimes wafts from the north down the valley along the Bluestone across Clover Bottom and on to the Mercer County seat.

Why were the Clay daughters not told the full version of the attack on Mitchell and Phoebe Belcher Clay's children? Why was Tabitha's bravery not passed down? Why were Tabitha's attempt to protect her brother, her frantic fight with the Indian who was about to scalp Bartley, her repeated grabs at the long, slashing knife not recounted? Why did no one speak of Phoebe's courage, the courage it took to walk toward those two disfigured bodies of her own children and drag them to her bed? Why was Tabitha and Phoebe's story told to David Johnston but not to the Clay girl-children, who could have used their courage as models for our own life crises?

I think I know the answer. It lies with a new family storyteller, the wife of William Clay—Mitchell and Phoebe Belcher's son— and my great-great-great-grandmother, Rebecca Cecil. After Rebecca Cecil married William Clay in April 1800, she became the keeper of the family stories, the filter, the one who determined what should be passed down to her children and grandchildren. And to Rebecca the Clays were not nearly as interesting, nor as important, as her own family, the Cecils.

Perhaps that is why the anguish of Rebecca Cecil's mother-in-law was never disclosed, never even alluded to—only the statue by the courthouse was noted, the statue that signified status. Instead, the Clay daughters—now Cecil daughters—were told stories about women who valued their possessions more than their children, who controlled their husbands with temper and threats. Our role models came from the stories of women who, if all else failed, either burned down houses or simply went upstairs to their bedrooms for a year to read and sip homemade wine while their children fended for themselves below. How meager were these stories—told so casually—how inadequate to teach us strength and character.

6

THE VOICE

I HAVE NO visual images connected to my great-great-great-grandmother Rebecca Cecil Clay, but her voice has hovered close to my ear most of my life. I cannot picture a house she lived in. No furniture that belonged to her has been passed to me, no small side table with delicately turned legs, no footstool, no mirror with a gold-leaf frame. I own no jewelry that was hers, nor a comb or a brush with an engraved handle or a slender silver tray for favorite earrings or collar pins. All I own are her words. And those words played a major role in my decision to flee Kentucky and the family. I did not like what Rebecca Cecil Clay had to say.

Rebecca Cecil Clay had only one story in the family canon: Rebecca was a Cecil. In the true sense of a story that has a beginning, a middle, and an end, this is no story at all. It is no story unless you see Rebecca as the pivot point in a protracted family saga that began in England and continues to this moment.

Rebecca entwined the Cecil and the Clay DNA. In 1800 she married William Clay, the son of Mitchell and Phoebe Clay who at age five saw his brother and sister killed, the son who half ran, half crawled on his short legs as he tearfully tried to keep up with his mother and his older brothers and sisters who were lunging through the woods toward the Baileys'. When William Clay married Rebecca Cecil on that early spring day in the rich valleys of southwestern Virginia, the saga of the Clay family changed. As a dowry Rebecca brought to the marriage the unshakable belief that "the Clays may have come over first, but the Cecils carried the aristocratic blood."

While the Clays and the Belchers and the Baileys migrated toward the mountains in southwest Virginia, the Cecils and the Wittens traveled in their own kinship group toward the same hills and valleys. They came from Maryland, most recently Fredericktown—now Frederick, Maryland, north and west of present-day Washington. That is not where the Cecil family originally settled, however. When John Baptist Cecil—the first Cecil to live and die in America—came to Maryland in 1658, he landed at St. Mary's on the tip of Maryland that is divided from Virginia by the Potomac River.

Unlike Virginia, which was chartered as a land investment company, Maryland was owned by a single family, the Calverts of Ireland. In 1631 George Calvert, 1st Baron Baltimore, had been granted land by his friend King Charles 1—ten million acres that stretched along the Atlantic between Virginia and the growing Dutch settlements to the north. George Calvert's desire was to found a Catholic community in America. Sadly, he died before he could take possession of his holdings and his dream of a safe haven for Catholics. Still, the land stayed in Calvert hands, passing to his son Cecilius Calvert, 2nd Baron Baltimore. Cecilius sent his younger brother Leonard Calvert to the new colony in 1633 to act as governor. Thomas Cecil, John Baptist Cecil's father, was among the two hundred passengers who left with Leonard Calvert from the Isle of Wight in November 1633 and arrived in Maryland in February 1634.

Thomas Cecil—spelled "Cecill" then—had not sailed on that first voyage to Maryland to start a new life on the Chesapeake. Instead, Thomas Cecil joined the colonists on assignment. He had been commissioned to make the first map of the new colony. Thomas Cecil was the natural choice to chart the new colony. He was an artist of reputation, well known at court. He was the son of Thomas Cecil, 1st Earl of Exeter, and grandson of William Cecil, Lord Burghley, forty-year friend and advisor to Elizabeth 1. Further, his uncle, Robert Cecil, 1st Earl of Salisbury half-brother to Thomas's father—was influential in the court, a supporter of England's colonization of America and a charter investor in the Virginia Company.

So when Thomas's son John Baptist Cecil came to Maryland in 1658, he came to oversee the land his father had been granted by the Calverts in payment for making that first map of Maryland. Born in England in 1638, John Baptist Cecil was only twenty when he emigrated. That same year he married Mary Calvert. There, in Maryland, John Baptist and Mary Calvert Cecil—joined later by at least one of John Cecil's brothers—put down roots. First the Cecils acquired land in St. Mary's New Town Hundred, later in Queen Anne's Parish and Prince George's County, and finally in Fredericktown. It was from there in northern Maryland around 1765 that Samuel Witten Cecil, John Baptist and Mary Calvert Cecil's great-grandson, decided to venture to the Virginia frontier. He was not alone. He and his wife, Rebecca White, and their children traveled with the Witten family.

The Wittens, like the Cecils, had been early colonizers in Maryland. Tradition puts the Wittens in the first group of settlers to come over with Leonard Calvert. Thomas Witten—our direct line—was born in England in 1632. On December 31, 1656, at age twenty-four he married Mary Bulkeley in Christ Church, Barbados, and the couple moved on to St. Mary's, Maryland. One generation later the Wittens and the Cecils began to marry.

The first of the Cecil-Witten marriages took place around 1719 when Ann Cecil—the granddaughter of John Baptist and Mary Calvert Cecil—married Thomas Witten. Thomas was the son of Thomas and Mary Buckeley Witten. Shortly after the marriage Thomas Jefferson Witten was born. It is here—with the birth of the third generation of Wittens in Maryland—that the stage was set for the future alliance of the Clays with the Cecil-Witten clan.

As the story goes, around 1765 Thomas Jefferson Witten and his brother-in-law Samuel Witten Cecil decided to move from Maryland to Virginia's newly opened territory in the southwest. With them were Thomas Jefferson's brothers James and Jerry Witten and each of their families. Like the Clays, the group stopped for a year in Bedford County—now Giles—to get their bearings. At first the families settled on Walkers Creek between Poplar Hill and White Gate. Although the Cecils stayed in Bedford County, the Witten brothers decided to move on.

Thomas Jefferson, James, and Jerry Witten moved south and west to Tazewell County, Virginia. They spread out along the Clinch River and Plum Creek at Crab Orchard near current-day Tazewell, where Thomas Jefferson built the first blockhouse in the area. Like Mitchell Clay, they fought in Dunmore's War from Fincastle County in 1774—and brought the first slaves into the region.

I do not know whether the Clays and the Cecil-Witten clan met in Bedford County or farther west. All I know is that on April 1, 1800, Rebecca Cecil and William Clay married in Montgomery County, Virginia. No one could have been better cast to play the celebrated family role of the heroine who carried the Cecil bloodline to the Clays of Virginia and Kentucky, for Rebecca carried an inordinate number of Cecil genes. The Cecils and the Wittens had begun to intermarry before leaving Maryland. In 1766, when the Cecils and the Wittens moved west together toward the newly opened regions of southwest Virginia, the families were tightly intermingled. Thomas Jefferson Witten was married to Samuel Cecil's sister, Elizabeth. Elizabeth was also the cousin of her mother-in-law, Ann Cecil Witten.

Perhaps it was the sparseness of the population in those far western Virginia counties, or perhaps it was simply familiarity. Whatever the reason, after the move from Maryland to southwest Virginia, the Cecils and the Wittens continued to intermarry. Five of Thomas and Elizabeth Cecil Witten's children married Samuel and Rebecca White Cecil's children—their double first cousins. One of those couplings was John Cecil and Keziah Witten, Rebecca's parents.

Here then was Rebecca Cecil, the star in the Clay-Cecil family drama, Rebecca who saw herself first and foremost as a Cecil. Not only was she a Cecil from her father's side of the family, she was a Cecil from her mother's side as well. Her Witten grandmother was a Cecil, her Witten grandfather was half Cecil. In Rebecca's mind she was not half Witten, half Cecil. She was all Cecil. She was the inheritor of the Cecil birthright, and with that inheritance came a responsibility: all of her progeny must know and value what it meant to be a Cecil, what it meant to be an aristocrat.

I am convinced that the eight generations that separated Rebecca from her famous and worldly lineal ancestor, William Cecil, Lord Burghley, were only moments to her. In her mind she, too, had served in Queen Elizabeth's court. She, too, had been the prized advisor and friend to a queen and, consequently, she knew the rules of the court, the courtly manners. She knew that "you cannot make a silk purse out of a sow's ear." She knew that a Lady never rolls back her sleeves; that a Lady does not do her own hand laundry, dust a table, wash a dish; she knew that birthright mattered above all else and that, whatever the circumstance, "a Lady of good birth" always handles herself with class.

When Rebecca Cecil married William Clay, the emphasis changed in our family stories. Stories about the first five generations of Clays on America's soil relayed the pride the Clays took in their early colonizing and their ongoing land acquisitions. They told of movement west across Virginia, of first white settlers in "western" territories. They taught the family children about the battles that were fought in our country's early history and the role the Clays played in Bacon's Rebellion, in the French and Indian War, in Dunmore's War, in the War of the Revolution.

After Rebecca joined the family, the men lost their leading roles in the stories. Their feats were no longer of prime importance; in fact, the lives of the men became nearly inconsequential in the family tales. The stories shifted to the lives of the women— women who carried the Cecil blood. Even though the men who married these Cecil women were civic leaders, legislators, and judges, from families of note in their own right, the successes of these men no longer mattered in the greater family saga. The main role of these men was to sire the children who would continue the Cecil bloodline, and, in order to ensure a sturdy bloodline, the family turned its attention to "good breeding."

In the North, the Midwest, and the West I imagine generations of children have never heard of good breeding outside a barnyard or a racetrack. In the South good breeding and family bloodlines are common topics at the dinner table: Family X has never had a problem with mental illness. Alcoholism runs in family Y. Family Z has never been able to hang onto its money. Or my favorite: His grandmother on his mother's side was a woods colt. Translation: His grandmother was illegitimate and you cannot be certain about the bloodline. After Rebecca, generations of the Cecil children—especially the girls—were educated with object lessons such as these.

Although each of the daughters in the family was thought to have married "beneath herself"—no blood could be as good as the Cecil blood—the family line surged forward. The men accepted the role of nurturing the family children and were heralded in the family annals, not as the accomplished professionals they were but as loving fathers. Those same men, however, were rarely mentioned as husbands—and when they were it was usually in complaint. The corporal corroboration of this attitude takes an odd form. After Rebecca Cecil, no woman in my direct family line has been buried next to her husband. Instead each chose to spend eternity with her mother, whom, if the stories are true, she never much liked.

With Rebecca Cecil as the pivot point, the structure of the family changed from a patriarchal to a matriarchal one, and the structure of the stories reflects the shift. The transformation comes through in a subtle but telling fashion in the naming of the leading characters in the family recollections. From Rebecca on, no female member of the family was referred to in a story by her married name; each was known only by her maiden name. Rebecca Cecil was never called Rebecca Cecil Clay, only Rebecca

Cecil. Rebecca's daughter was not identified by her well-known husband's name, Burns, only as Kizzie Clay. Kizzie's daughter, Catharine Rebecca Burns Mott, was always Kate Burns. Birthname designations were even superimposed on the past. Henry Clay's wife is referenced in seventeenth- and eighteenth-century documents as Mary Clay. The family called her Mary Mitchell. Phoebe Clay was known to me only as Phoebe Belcher. Ours was now a matriarchal line in name and in spirit.

What about William Clay? Where was he while Rebecca Cecil was redefining the family story? He was never mentioned in the family. He had no story of his own—just that he married Rebecca. He—like each of the husbands who married the "Cecil women"—lost his identity. Yet, according to my research, William did what each of the Clay men before him had done. He reshaped and maintained the region where he lived. He was a member of the local militia. Eventually he followed his Cecil in-laws through the gaps in the Appalachian Mountains down the Tug Fork of the Big Sandy River to the small but well-situated merchant settlement of Louisa, Kentucky. There he raised his Cecil children. I knew none of their names until recently. None except for my great-great-grandmother Keziah—named for her grandmother Keziah Witten who was also a Cecil.

Rebecca's Cecil-ness was repellent to me. Whenever one of her sayings was repeated I felt shame. By age eleven I had determined that I did not want to live in a town where everyone knew my family tree, knew that I was a Clay and a Cecil and—most frightening—thought that my ancestry mattered, that it defined me.

I am not certain why I wanted ancestral anonymity when the rest of the family felt protected by the marquee of our well-bred bloodline. All I know is that I am still trying to unravel my issues with ancestry. On the other hand, my great-great-grandmother Keziah—Rebecca Cecil and William Clay's youngest child—had no argument with her mother's arrogant ancestral attitudes. She lived the family dictum of "class above all" with one horrifying exception. No one shared that one example of outrageous behavior with me until I was in my forties. Her story is next.

7

HOUSE STORIES

EZIAH BYCE "Kizzie" Clay Burns, my great-great-grand-mother, must have made her mother proud. Not only did Kizzie Clay wear her Cecil-ness with head held arrogantly high, she passed on Rebecca Cecil's dictums regarding Cecil woman-hood to the family daughters with such certainty and precision that Rebecca's words were etched in the psyches of the next four generations. Throughout her life Kizzie Clay wore her famous birthright like a cloak of courtly damask. She, like her mother, never forgot that she was a direct descendent of William Cecil, Lord Burghley. She knew she was a lady of good breeding and she expected—no, demanded—to be treated as such.

For much of her life Kizzie's expectations were met, including a fairytale courtship with a handsome young prince. This story about Kizzie's courtship and marriage—a period that may have been one of the happiest in Kizzie's life—was never told, how-ever, from the young bride's blissful point of view. Rather, the story—like all of our courtship stories that followed—was told from the viewpoint of a family that prized its bloodlines.

Kizzie's whirlwind romance began when strikingly handsome John Mavity Burns came to call. It was early 1843 in Louisa, Kentucky, where William and Rebecca Cecil Clay now lived. John was nineteen. Kizzie was fifteen. The courtship was brief. Kizzie alleged to her daughter and granddaughters that it was love at first sight, and the two were married on April 24, 1843. The family saw the betrothal through a darker lens. The problem: John Burns was too handsome.

John had dark wavy hair, deep-set dark blue eyes, a chiseled jaw, and full, lush lips. In contrast, Kizzie was homely. She looked like the Clays. Her face was anvil-shaped, her nose was too long, her lips made a tight, thin line. So—and this is the crux of Kizzie's fairytale-marriage story as seen through the family's eyes—the family asked itself about the motive for this courtship. Why did handsome John Burns pick out homely Kizzie Clay when he could marry any young woman in eastern Kentucky? And the family answered its own question: John married Kizzie because she was a Cecil and a Clay. He married her for her family connections. After all, said the family, at the time of the courtship Kizzie's cousin, Henry Clay, was once again running for president. Another cousin, Cassius Marcellus Clay, in his thirties in 1843, was already a noted spokesman on abolitionist issues, an advisor to political leaders across the country on issues of slavery.

There may have been some truth to the family conclusion, for John Burns was an ambitious young man. Yet choosing Kizzie as his bride could not have been all about her family connections. John Burns came from a well-connected Virginia and Kentucky family himself. His great-grandfather and great-uncle came from Scotland in the seventeenth century—first to Maryland, then across Virginia to the Commonwealth's fledgling southwest territory, and finally into Kentucky. Jerome Burns, John's Revolutionary War grandfather, was a noted Methodist preacher as well as a legislator. John's father, Roland Tiernan Burns, was one of the first settlers in Boyd County, Kentucky, and both his and John's uncles were lawyers and legislators. John's brother had a thriving law practice in Louisa where John was apprenticing when he met Kizzie. John Burns's background and good qualities were overlooked, however, in the seismic story-shift from patriarchy to matriarchy that occurred in our family saga after Rebecca Cecil married William Clay.

Although Kizzie's romantic courtship was disparaged by the family, her next story was told with immense pride. Once again the story, allegedly about Kizzie, was really about something else altogether. This time it was about a house. It was about a house John built for Kizzie in Prestonsburg, Kentucky, a house that was so gracious and so elegant that it was known as "the finest house in town." It, in fact, was so superior to the other houses in Prestonsburg that Colonel James A. Garfield of the Eighteenth Brigade of Ohio commandeered it for his headquarters during the Civil War Battle of Middle Creek. And—the storyteller would pause here for dramatic emphasis—future President Garfield liked the house so much that he came back after the war and bought it.

The story takes place eighteen years after John and Kizzie's wedding. By this time there are six children. Nine years earlier the couple had moved to Prestonsburg on the Levisa Fork of the Big Sandy River to further John's political ambitions. Prestonsburg, the major town in Floyd County, was the political center of eastern Kentucky, the place for a young attorney to build a career. Kizzie had not wanted to leave her Clay and Cecil relatives in gracious Louisa for raucous, ill-kept Prestonsburg, but John bribed her by promising to build her the finest house in town, built to her vision of what the home of a Cecil should be.

The promised house stood on a rise high above the steeply sloping banks of the Levisa Fork of the Big Sandy. It was grand in size, two stories, painted white—built from the abundance of hardwood available in the surrounding hills. Perfectly proportioned double columns framed the stately doors and supported porches on both the ground and veranda levels. The rooms were spacious with high ceilings and graceful woodwork, the windows were tall and shuttered, and the fireplaces had elegant mantles. It was a fine house.

The move to Prestonsburg had paid off for John. By the time Garfield's Ohio Brigade was sent to eastern Kentucky to push the Confederates back into Virginia, John had served in the Kentucky legislature and had been elected to a judgeship that covered most of the eastern part of the state. He was, in fact, sitting on the bench in Mount Sterling in central Kentucky when Garfield commandeered Kizzie's house. According to Kizzie—who was noted in the family as a complainer—"John was always away." It was normal, wretchedly normal, that she was left to deal with everything on her own, including Garfield and his troops.

So, according to the story, here Kizzie was, alone except for her sixteen-year-old son, Roland Clay Burns. To make matters worse, she was sick. She had a lingering deep cough that she had not been able to shake throughout the rainy winter. She was too weak to climb the stairs to her bedroom and lay on a daybed in the everyday sitting room when she heard the earsplitting bangs on her heavy front door. It was the morning of January 11, 1862, a day of icy rain in the wettest winter in Big Sandy River Valley memory.

The rifle-butt bangs continued until Kizzie slowly made her way from the daybed to the door. Three of Garfield's soldiers informed Kizzie that they needed her house for Garfield's command center and that she and Roland could stay if they wanted. Even though she was too sick to stand alone, she would not stay. Kizzie did not trust these Union troops, even though she and John were the only northern sympathizers in Prestonsburg. She did not trust them because they took her gold watch—the one her mother, Rebecca, had given her—and all the money she had in the house, seventeen dollars.

Kizzie knew when the scouts left that she did not have long before Garfield and his officers would return. Clinging to Roland's arm, she—like so many Southern women who lived through the Civil War—gathered up the family treasures: the sterling silver, the tea service and candlesticks, the mint julep cups, and as many of the Clay and Cecil mementos and pieces of jewelry as she could stuff into heavy linen pillowcases. Roland hurriedly wrapped the bags in burlap and buried them in the garden. By the time Roland had covered Kizzie's precious treasures with manure, his mother had collapsed. So Roland ran for help.

According to the family story, just moments before Garfield's troops overran Prestonsburg, Roland—with help from a friend—carried Kizzie down the steep embankment in front of their house and lifted her into the family's flat-bottomed boat. Then, placing her on a pallet, the two boys wrapped her in quilts to protect her from the freezing drizzle. The weeks of steady rain produced a swift current in the Levisa Fork of the Big Sandy, which helped Roland pole his mother sixty miles downriver to his Grandmother Rebecca's in Louisa. By the time Roland got to Louisa, Kizzie was burning with fever and unable to speak.

But that was not the end of the story. There was simply a pause in the action. We all—the children—caught our breath while Kizzie recuperated. When Kizzie was well and after the troops had moved on to other battlefields, Rebecca Cecil's daughter made an announcement to husband, children, and mother. She would not return to Prestonsburg. She refused, she said, to ever set foot in that house again. The reason Keziah Byce Clay Burns gave—and always the storyteller's closing line in the tale was the same—was this: "Those soldiers had tramped all over the house in their muddy boots. It will never be clean again."

Kizzie stuck to her decision. January 11, 1862—the day Colonel James A. Garfield and the officers of the Eighteenth Brigade of Ohio commandeered her house—was the last day Kizzie ever spent in the house that she loved so much, the house that perfectly fit her vision of what it meant to be a lady of good breeding. She did not want to see the house after the Battle of Middle Creek. No one in the family, including John Burns, seemed to question her decision. When I asked my grandmother how Kizzie could do such a thing, how she could leave this special house forever, my grandmother said about her grandmother: "It was just the way Kizzie was. It was just Kizzie."

Still, I always found the muddy boots part of Kizzie's house story peculiar. I knew that the women in the family passionately loved their houses. And I knew that some of us, including myself, were obsessed with clean floors. But how much mud could there be? How much mud would it take to feel you could never again face your beloved house? My questions were answered the day I walked past a volume set of President James A. Garfield's papers in the Newberry Library and stopped short.

Since I am a historian—a detective of sorts—my heart has never ceased doing a fluttering foxtrot when I sense I might be on to a clue to past mysteries. When I saw the collection of Garfield's papers in the Newberry Library, I sensed I was on to something.

I knew there could be primary data in those heavy volumes that would corroborate the family's oral history concerning Garfield and Kizzie's house. I took a deep breath and began to scan the letters and military communiqués that Garfield wrote during the war years.

It was all there. There were communiqués that confirmed the family accounts of the heavy rains that fell that January 1862. There were others that described the difficulty of supplying the troops because of the brisk current in the Levisa Fork of the Big Sandy River—the river that ran beside Kizzie's house with the heavy current that helped Roland pole downriver toward Rebecca Cecil's house in Louisa. In another communiqué Garfield told his commander that he sent three soldiers ahead to find a house in Prestonsburg suitable for his headquarters during the Battle of Middle Creek—the soldiers who took Kizzie's watch and her money.

And then I found this:

Headquarters Eighteenth Brigade, Prestonsburg, Kentucky

January 11, 1862.

I left Paintsville on Thursday noon with 1,100 men, and drove in the enemy's pickets 2 miles beyond Prestonsburg. The men slept on their arms. At 4 o'clock yesterday morning we moved toward the main body of the enemy at the Forks of Middle Creek. . . . The enemy burned most of his stores and fled precipitately.

Today I have crossed the river, and am now occupying Prestonsburg. Our loss 2 killed and 25 wounded.

J. A. Garfield
Colonel, Commanding Brigade

I felt a surge of excitement and—I have to admit despite my former disdain for the stories—a spark of pride. I pictured future President James A. Garfield sitting at my great-great-grandmother's desk in her elegant living room with the oriental rugs and the gracious curves of the couch that John had sent to Prestonsburg by water from Louisville—the couch that is horribly uncomfortable but still moves down generations of family living rooms because it is "Kizzie Clay's couch." I wondered if Garfield had already begun to be taken by this house, had already decided that he would come back after the war and try to buy it. I sat staring out at the treetops through the tall Palladian windows of the library imagining the scene, then looked down at the next entry and caught my breath.

Included in Garfield's papers regarding the Battle of Middle Creek was a letter he wrote to his wife concerning the early morning of January 10, 1862. In the midst of the letter was this passage:

> *At half past twelve o'clock I climbed the hill and rolled myself up in a blanket, while the cold, drizzling rain poured down upon us during the whole night. At three in the morning I turned out and called up the boys to take their crackers and prepare for the march. I assure you it was a very dreary prospect. The deepest, worst mud I ever saw was under foot, and a dense cold fog hung around us as the boys filed slowly down the hillside . . .*

The family's description of the "wettest winter in Big Sandy River Valley memory" was true. The "icy drizzle" in the story was true. And the amount of mud that must have been tracked into Kizzie's house was true. The family had not elaborated the details to make the story worth telling. Nor did the storytellers exaggerate Garfield's fondness for Kizzie's fine home. He did go back to Prestonsburg after the war to buy it, and from then on it was called "Garfield House."

By the time I made my way to Prestonsburg, Kizzie's house had been torn down to make way for a bank. Pictures of the house, however, hung in Billy Ray's Restaurant just doors away. During lunch I asked the waitress about "Garfield House." She directed me to a table of older locals who vied with one another to give me a full account of the house's history: "Used to belong to Judge John Burns way back"—"married a Clay," someone offered—"but he sold it after the war." "That's when President Garfield bought it. Garfield never spent a day in it after the Battle of Middle Creek. Got assassinated. Didn't live long enough to enjoy it. It was a fine house. You a relative? Too bad you didn't get to see it. It was a fine house. Would've made you proud."

After Kizzie left Prestonsburg, she stayed in Louisa with her mother and younger children. When the Confederates attempted to capture Louisa in spring 1863, she was too frightened to stay much longer. John was practicing law and speaking around the state on education issues. In 1864 he was appointed Boyd County Commissioner of Schools and moved from Prestonsburg to Catlettsburg, Boyd County's county seat. Since Catlettsburg was only twenty-five easy downriver miles from the Clays and Cecils in Louisa, Kizzie decided to rejoin her husband. She asked John to find a house that would suit her. John succeeded.

Kizzie's new home was large and elegant and directly across the brick-paved street from the courthouse. The house met the standards for the wife of a prominent lawyer and commissioner and, for the first time in years, Kizzie Clay spent time with her husband. She felt safe, she had her fine house, she was contented. According to the family, Kizzie Clay's pleasure in her big house in Catlettsburg, where she entertained jurists and politicians in fine Cecil style, lasted for a decade. Then the whispers began, whispers about her husband and another woman. No one would tell her at first, but finally Kizzie Clay demanded to know and her friends told her about Josephine.

Throughout Kizzie's marriage, John stayed away from home for extended periods. Sometimes he was in Frankfort where he represented his district in the legislature. Other times he rode the circuit throughout eastern Kentucky. In his travels he purchased properties. One of these purchases was a chicken farm not far from Catlettsburg. The tenant who lived on the property and ran the farm was Josephine Chrisman. What most of Catlettsburg knew and had known for years was that John had been living with Josephine whenever possible. To make matters worse, John and Josephine had two daughters shockingly, scandalously, unbelievably named after two of his legitimate daughters: Kate and Cora Lee.

Kizzie had to know if these whispered rumors were true. According to the story, which I did not hear until I was in my forties, one night when John did not return for dinner, Kizzie hitched the horse to the carriage and headed toward Josephine's house. The night was windy, the story goes, and the moon lit the way for just moments at a time as the clouds rushed by. Having grown up where Kizzie's drama unfolds, I can picture what that trip was like. I know how the clouds lie low in the valleys, and I can feel the sharp cracking vibrations of the river as the wind slaps it against the bank beside the carriage path. I can feel deep inside my chest the mournful vibrations of the foghorns that still direct the coal and lumber barges between the banks of the Big Sandy and down the Ohio.

As Kizzie rounds the last bend in the path, she sees Josephine's house. John's horse is tethered to the porch railing. As the tension built in the story, I whispered to Mother with apprehension, "What did she do when she saw he was there?" Mother replied with calm matter-of-factness, "She burned the house down." "She what!" I yelped in shock at both the act of arson and the composed way it was related. "She burned the house down," Mother repeated serenely, as if this were a totally acceptable consequence of John's unfaithfulness. And was just the way Kizzie was.

Josephine Chrisman, John Burns, and their two daughters escaped out the back door of the frame house before the fire, whipped by the high night winds, burned it to the ground. John did not press charges. Kizzie divorced her husband. It was 1874, the first of the family's divorces—except for Kizzie's cousin, Cassius Clay, who had publicly separated from his wife of fifty years five years previously and would divorce her four years hence.

On June 11, 1875—thirteen years and five months to the day after Colonel James A. Garfield requisitioned Kizzie's fine house in Prestonsburg—John married Josephine Chrisman. Their two daughters, Kate and Cora Lee, stood up as witnesses at the wedding of their parents. The family always referred to Josephine Chrisman Burns as "Ole Jose" and acknowledged her sweetness and kindness—something even Kizzie's children felt their mother had been incapable of providing their father.

After the divorce Kizzie stayed in the fine house in Catlettsburg across the street from the courthouse where John would soon preside—despite the scandal—and where his portrait was later hung to mark his Circuit Court service to the region. On her deathbed Kizzie asked for him. John Mavity Burns—former Representative and Senator, Circuit Court Judge of Kentucky's

Sixteenth Judicial District, and "Ole Jose's" husband—held his former wife's hand as she died on October 18, 1896.

Kizzie's stories—the ones chosen by the storytellers to define her—were told as examples to the daughters that followed. There was, however, one story about Kizzie that was never openly discussed. The script was so minimal that we daughters only learned the story from our mothers through body language—a pantomime that played out gradually and in bits and pieces. Despite its limited libretto, the subtext of this story had more impact on us than all of Kizzie's other stories. It was about Kizzie's attitude toward her children. My great-great-grandmother did not like to mother.

Kizzie was the first of the Cecil mothers who we know for sure was unable to reach out to her children, and the first who preferred her sons over her daughters. She was the first of the mothers in the family to rely on her husband to provide affection and nurturing to her offspring, and the first to pick out with uncanny prescience a mate who could offset her own reserve. For the next four generations the daughters-who-would-be-mothers learned distance at their mothers' knees. Phoebe Belcher Clay's tears over the deaths of her cherished children were no longer part of our repertoire. We were Cecil mothers now.

The storytellers—mothers all—made light of Kizzie's mothering style. Another reality, however, crept into the pages of diaries and letters of Kizzie's offspring, reinforced by the remoteness the girl-children sensed in their own mothers. Although we despaired of the detachment, felt diminished by it, we were given no tools to treat our own daughters in any other way. We were, however, given our fathers.

The family may have doubted handsome John Burns's motives when he came to court young homely Kizzie Clay. Kizzie, on the other hand, even at age fifteen, seemed to have recognized something in John. John was a nurturer and an enabler. If Kizzie wanted a fine house, he would build it. If she wanted fine furniture, he would buy it in cosmopolitan Cincinnati or Louisville and have it shipped along Kentucky's winding waterways into the remote mountains of eastern Kentucky. If she did not want to take care of their children, he would make sure there was someone who did. And he showered his children with affection. John became the prototype for husbands and fathers to follow.

Rebecca Cecil Clay was the pivot point in our family, who turned our oral history away from the actions of our forefathers and directed the family chronicle toward the lives of our foremothers. Keziah Byce Clay Burns, Rebecca's devoted daughter, solidified the slant of the new era. We learned that we were strong, that we could look into the eyes of soldiers without fear, that we could hide the family treasures, that we could handle difficult situations without husbands. Conversely, Kizzie's stories also gave us permission to be demanding and headstrong. We could insist on fine houses and the furniture that went in them and expect to receive it. We could make willful decisions and refuse to reconsider them.

We learned by the tone of the telling that it was acceptable under certain circumstances to act impetuously, it was alright to burn down a house in anger if the situation called for it. But we also learned how to spot men who would take up the slack if we fell prey to the Cecil-mother syndrome. We listened well, and we reenacted Kizzie's stories with different husbands and other houses. We were Cecil women now. And that's the way we thought life was.

8

DADDY'S GIRL

ATHARINE REBECCA "Kate" Burns, my great-grandmother, was Kizzie Clay and John Burns's first child, born in July 1844, barely fifteen months after the couple's fairytale courtship and wedding. The baby was named after her two grandmothers, Catharine Keyser Burns and Rebecca Cecil Clay. Kizzie called her daughter Rebecca to remind her that she was a Cecil, but John refused to call her anything but Kate.

The fact that Kate chose for herself the name her father preferred reflects more than a personal preference on Kate's part. It reflects the family dynamic in the Burns household. Kate was her father's child. Until she reached her mid-twenties her life was so intertwined with that of her father that his stories were hers and hers, his. John Burns adored and pampered Kate and her character was shaped accordingly. Kate was bright and social, yet she was also arrogant and selfish. Kate was above all else self-centered, and her stories reflected that part of her nature.

My grandmother, Kate's youngest child, always said that she and her sisters knew from early on that their mother liked her house more than she liked her children—with perhaps the exception of her only living son, Glen Ford, whom the sisters secretly called "the Crown Prince." They also knew that Kate had been spoiled by her father and then by theirs. That knowledge did not diminish the power of the stories about Kate's behavior when life did not go her way. Kate's stories wrapped themselves around the rest of us. Although some of us struggled against the entanglement, Kate's stories inexorably became our own.

By the time Kate was born, John Burns was an attorney riding the circuit in eastern Kentucky. The family liked to recount how "John had his Kate on a horse when she could scarcely sit a saddle." From then on Kate—and the servant girl who took care of Kate throughout her young life—traveled with John as he followed the court circuit and politicked from the mountainous border with Virginia to the edge of the Bluegrass region in central Kentucky. In 1857, when Kate was thirteen, John was elected to the Kentucky legislature representing Floyd and Johnson counties. Kizzie Clay stayed in Prestonsburg in the fine house John had built for her four years earlier. Kate and "her girl" moved to Frankfort in central Kentucky with her father.

This period in Kate's life when she served as her father's hostess was exhilarating. She loved to reminisce with my mother about that time in Frankfort, about the political discussions she was privy to, about the tensions that flared as the country inalterably moved toward the Civil War. Mother liked to tell me Kate's stories of those sparkling formative years. When she talked about that period in Kate's life I watched Mother ease back into a time when her beloved "Gram" was still alive, when she and her grand-

mother furtively sipped Kate's homemade wine and smoked cigarettes in front of the fire in Kate's fine house.

I have vivid images of that period in my great-grandmother's
life. My pictures of Kate's experiences in Frankfort, however, do
not come solely from Mother's stories. Instead, they come from
an object—a small pine box with a smooth hand-carved wooden
handle attached to the flat top by irregularly shaped square-topped
nails. The carrying case—for that is what it really is, even though I
have known it all my life as "the trunk Kate took to Frankfort"—is
twenty inches long and ten inches wide and deep. An inch-wide
black metal band wraps around the box lengthwise, strapping the
four sides together. A heavy latch swings down to fasten top to
bottom and to lock in the trunk's belongings with a long-lost delicate brass key. The pine of Kate's trunk has turned a deep persimmon red with age. The linen strip that holds the lid upright when
opened has frayed and yellowed with age, and I no longer trust it
to do its job. The paper that lines the interior has browned around
the edges and is stained in spots from small spills, but the stylized
pattern of dainty yellow and green flowerets remains clear.

Through this small case, which has been mine for as long as
I can remember, I have lived an enchanted life with my great-
grandmother. I have traveled on horseback through the hills of
eastern Kentucky. I have ridden in a post carriage on the Old
Pound Gap Road cut roughly through the mountains from Virginia, past Prestonsburg to Mount Sterling on the edge of central
Kentucky. I have crossed the rolling hills of the Bluegrass region
through miles and miles of land owned by Green Clay and then
by Cassius and his brothers, past Henry Clay's estate, Ashland,
in Lexington and on toward the deep cut of the Kentucky River
and the state's capitol in Frankfort. I can picture Kate and her girl

with this small pine box and feel her excitement as she walks into her father's lodgings in Frankfort and later up the long stairs to her room at Science Hill Academy.

When John Burns first settled in Frankfort he enrolled Kate in Greenville Seminary. Soon, however, he moved her to Shelbyville—twenty miles by good road from Frankfort—to attend Science Hill Academy. At Science Hill, Kate took a formal college preparatory curriculum: courses in language skills, mathematics, the sciences—"including astronomy," the recitation always went—and French, as well as the usual refinement classes for "young ladies of good breeding" in music and art. She also formed friendships with young women sent to Science Hill from every state in the Union. According to Kate, those early—and lasting—friendships changed her, gave her a vision that extended beyond the mountains of eastern Kentucky and the Big Sandy River valley.

I went to Shelbyville a few years ago to see the reality of my imagined stay at the Science Hill Academy with Kate and her little trunk. My romantic imaginings were not far off—perhaps because eighteenth- and nineteenth-century Kentucky architecture is part of my being. The school—now a restaurant and interior design shop—is a flat-fronted brick building painted white with a long side porch for wicker furniture and a wooden swing. As in most early Kentucky towns, homes and businesses were set close to the street, with gardens to the side or back. Science Hill follows that pattern. The school sides the street, but in the interior of the large U-shaped structure is an enclosed garden. Low prim boxwood hedges prescribe the pathways through the grounds while pedestal fountains and decorative wrought-iron benches dotted here and there among the hedges and trees break the formality. The kitchen opened onto the garden, and as

I walked along the paths I imagined the "young ladies of good breeding" ambling arm-in-arm as they judged suppertime from the aromas of food and the scraping and clinking sounds of cast-iron skillets and roasters that radiated through the wood-spooled screen door that was still there.

The inside of the academy outdid my imagination. In the center of the large rectangular space that joined the two side wings was an atrium flooded with light from a conservatory-glass ceiling. Classrooms and laboratories encircled the lower level. Above—up steep stairs—were the girls' rooms. A wide veranda swept around the upper space, allowing the boarders to gaze on the world below or to communicate in echoed stage whispers across the open air to friends on the other side. The space was magic. I could picture my great-grandmother laughing and whispering and hugging and kissing—for she was said to have been truly happy there, happier than at any other time in her life. And I could envision somewhere in that aerie Kate's small pine chest filled with trinkets and letters and the memory book her beloved father gave her in 1857.

For Christmas 1857—Kate's first year in Frankfort—John gave his daughter a keepsake album. The album, with its embossed leather covers and gold-tipped pages, is now mine. I pull it out sometimes just to look at the spidery nineteenth-century script written in fading brown ink. I feel the physical presence of our family when I read what Kate's brothers and sisters wrote. Roland Clay—years before he poled his feverish mother downstream away from Garfield's troops in Prestonsburg—and Milton Shakespeare Burns, Kate's young brothers, write in pencil. Roland has drawn slightly sloping lines on the page to keep his young penmanship straight. Milton Shakespeare writes a poem with a single stanza.

My life may be forever dark
And all my friends may flee
But in my hours of loneliness
I'll often think of thee.

Your Brother

Milton S. Burns

Sophia, Minerva, and Cora Lee, Kate's three sisters, write sonnets for Kate in perfect script. This album provides a window into the family's big house in Prestonsburg during that Christmas holiday—five winters before Garfield requisitioned the house, five years before Kizzie Clay turned her back on it.

Yet something is wrong. Each time I open the album and turn through it page by page, I can find no sentimental words to Kate from her mother. Sometimes I obsessively check to make sure I have not overlooked the greeting from Kizzie Clay. I carefully squeeze the front and back of each gold-tipped page between my thumb and forefinger, shifting slightly to make sure that no pages have somehow stuck together. I even suspiciously examine each quire to make sure that nothing has been carefully cut away from the binding. But even though the entries in Kate's keepsake album cover a period of eight years, during which Kate's father makes several entries, there is nothing in it from her mother.

Despite the lack of an affectionate relationship with her mother, Kate grew into a poised young woman in Frankfort and Shelbyville, mature beyond her years. She was of medium height and had the Clays' dark coloring, high cheekbones, and long, straight nose. Her mouth was rather thin, usually set in a straight line. In none of her pictures is she smiling—not even in the snapshots taken in her garden after the children had left home—a period in her life when, as in Frankfort, she was said to be happy. Still, her self-confidence and her dark eyes that, according to family lore, flashed black with delight or anger drew both men and women to her.

When she was twenty-two Kate moved from the arms of her father to those of James Ward from Louisa, Kentucky. On a May afternoon in 1866—when John's relationship with Josephine was still a secret from the family—Kate and James were married in the living room of John and Kizzie Clay's big house across from the courthouse in Catlettsburg. According to the story, James Ward was one of the few acceptable matches for a Cecil daughter. The Wards helped establish Louisa, Kentucky, the storyteller always proudly noted. In fact—and then there would be a pause for significance—the town was named for James Ward's mother, Louisa, the first baby born in the settlement.

Nine months after the marriage, Kate's first child was born and named Louisa as a reminder of her good Virginia and Kentucky stock. Seven months later, James Ward was killed on Election Day as he attempted to separate two quarreling drunks. To those of us who have vivid imaginations, the grim story was chillingly graphic. According to the story, James Ward had been shoved out of the way when he tried to stop the Election Day fight. He lost his balance and fell. James Ward hit his head against the edge of a wagon axle and "cracked his head open."

At the time of his death, James and Kate were living in Grayson, Kentucky, fifteen miles east of Catlettsburg. Late in her life in a codicil to her will Kate spoke about that day.

I have a mixed family and had one daughter by James Ward, seven months old whose father was killed. My dear father, Honorable J. M. Burns came out to Grayson, Kentucky, brought me

and my little infant daughter to his house in Catlettsburg. He
seen to the burial of my husband and paid funeral expenses as
we had no money but we owned a 2 horse-team and an ox-team
as he had contract from a sawmill plant near Grayson to deliver
timber to said plant there.

After the accident Kate remained in Catlettsburg to be near
her father and, on his advice, in August 1868 earned her certifi-
cation to teach in the Boyd County school system. By then the
romantic tale of Kate's marriage to handsome Dwight Hawkins
"Frank" Mott was just beginning.

Frank Mott was a widower with four children. His family
members originally were fur traders from upper New York State
and then Michigan. By the time Frank met Kate he was living in
Kentucky, where he supervised one of the largest lumber mills in
the region, buying and selling first-growth trees in Kentucky and
West Virginia and brokering mortgages on mountain timberland.
Frank was financially comfortable and his carousing days were
behind him—the family whispered that his first marriage may
have been a forced one. He was tall and handsome. He had dark
eyes, dark wavy hair, and high cheekbones—a holdover from his
Indian great-grandmother on his father's side. He was also a war
hero who had raised his own cavalry division in the 10th Regiment of Volunteer Cavalry—the 45th Kentucky Mounted Infantry—to fight for the Union. I loved my great-grandfather even
though he died long before I was born. I loved him because of a
story the family told time and again about his Civil War years.

As the story goes, Frank Mott was thirty-four in the summer
of 1862, and had dreamed about his favorite horse. He was uneasy
because whenever he dreamed of his horse, somebody died. This
time he was anxious about his men. There was a drought in cen-

tral Kentucky where his regiment was headquartered, and there had been no fresh water for a day. The horses were dying and his boys were suffering. He had to do something. So he took Captain Shockley, one of his men and the one who later told the story, and went in search of water. Although I know the story by heart and can see clearly each scene in my head, I will switch to the nineteenth-century account of what happened.

Fort Scott Record
May 1, 1885

WILL A SOLDIER PRAY?

Many amusing incidents occurred in the late passage of arms, between the North and the South, but none more so than the one that occurred to those two gallant captains, Frank Mott and Shockley of the 45th Kentucky mounted infantry. During the summer of 1862, a drouth had struck the country in which they were operating, and one whole day had passed with out man or beast tasting a single drop of water, or at least enough to quench their thirst. Grasping an old coffee pot, the two suffering men sallied forth in search of water. The dust in the road was ankle deep and hot to the feet. Across lots, all grass and vegetation was parched and literally burned to a crisp. A pool of water was observed in an old tobacco field in which lay the carcass of a Confederate mule. Hastening to the spot, a cup full of water alive with maggots, was scooped up and carried to the lips, but the nausea of the stomach from the putrid smell caused them to dash the filthy stuff to the ground. Despairing of relief they sought shelter in an old tobacco dry house. After a few moments of rest, Shockley noticed Captain Mott sliding off to himself and climbing up to the top story of the building. He felt sure that Captain

Mott was either losing his senses or determined to commit some desperate deed.

At last the sound of a pleading voice fell upon his ear; bracing himself against the side of the building what was Shockley's surprise to hear coming from the lips of this brave fearlessly dashing soldier, a prayer to God in behalf of the suffering soldier and his companion, the horse. Eloquent words, so earnest and yet so firmly believing:

"Great God of battles, help us today! Send now to our parched throats relief; open the sluice gates of Heaven and pour upon us a deluge of refreshing rain. Now do it, God; if you have any sympathy in your great heart, do not delay but pour it out."

A moment before this earnest appeal was offered, the sun shown out as clear, dry and crisp as it ever did. Before the captain had arisen from his knees, drop, drop, here and there, upon the curled up shingles was distinctly heard; faster and faster did it come, until at last a mighty roar was heard, as if every window in the heavens was opened, and a mighty deluge of water coming sure. What was the condition of the two men in the old dry house? Shockley stood in the center of the building hugging a post, white as a ghost, and trembling with fear, exclaimed: "Great God, Mott! What have you done? Has the judgment day come?" Mott by this time had descended from the loft and trembling and pale as Shockley was, replied, "Damfino, Shock."

These two brave men stood trembling, looking at each other, the rain pelting the old house until it made a roaring rumbling sound. These two men who dared to brave and storm the enemy's works and face death in a thousand ways, who were never known to quail before a storm of shot and shell and saber charge, were so badly scared over this little incident that they forgot to catch even a little drop of water that fell but let old Mother Earth drink it up and soak it away. In a few moments after the first drop fell, it stopped and two minutes thereafter the ground had not the slightest indication of having received a drop of water.

Captain Shockley is connected with the Van Fesson and Wilcox Loan Bank, and vouches for the truth of the above incident. Captain Mott is still alive and resides in Catlettsburg, Kentucky and had the reputation of being the bravest man in the regiment, and up to the above mentioned time, had scorned to bend a knee to any human being divine, from the time he left his mother's knee, until after this incident occurred.

Even though by this time in the family saga the stories starred the female members of the family, this anecdote about my great-grandfather contained many of the elements the family valued. There was the dream of the horse as omen. There was the resolution to take charge in a compromised situation. And there was the ironic ending, which would allow the participant in any family story in the making to quip, as we all do, "Well, at least it will make a good story." Because of each of those things Frank's tale made it through the female gauntlet and was passed on. Of greater significance in the family canon than Frank's war-years story, however, was this one: Frank adored his "black-eyed Kate," his "Little Black Baby Kate," and promised to build her the house of her dreams.

Frank and Kate married on July 7, 1869. She was twenty-five and he was forty-one. Soon Frank's four children and Little Lou Ward gained two sisters—Ida Lee and Lena Leota. Then Frank and Kate lost a baby boy—Baby Burns—but gained another—Glen Ford. Finally in 1886, when Kate was forty-two, she gave birth to one last unexpected and unwanted baby. She gave the baby girl—my grandmother—to Frank as soon as she was born and told him to name her, that she did not care what she was called. Frank named my grandmother Wynemah "after an Indian princess," he said, and called her his "Little Indian" for the rest of his life. Kate had found a man to nurture her children just as her mother Kizzie Clay had done.

Frank's promised gift to Kate—"the elegant gem of small-town splendor," as the house was referred to by family and friends—was in Ceredo, West Virginia. It was just across the river from Catlettsburg—where all of the children had been born—so Kate could still be near her father while Frank could be close to the lumber mill. The house sat on a corner lot of First Street facing the Congregational Church. Other rambling Victorian houses painted in grays or creams were set back in huge, clipped lawns on both sides of the street. Some of the houses had steeply gabled roofs, others deep wraparound porches; still others had tall turrets that lent a fairytale quality to the neighborhood. It was a wide street with first- and second-growth trees leaning into each other to twist and twine high overhead. It was a street of friendly neighbors, except for the Major Frank Waymer family next door, whom Frank Mott refused to acknowledge because the father and sons had sided with the Rebels in the War.

There in Ceredo on hot summer days, women sat in freshly painted wicker furniture to do handwork on porches with deep shady overhangs. Snowball hydrangea bushes backed up against the diamond-patterned trellises that wrapped around the houses, and hollyhocks in all shades of rosy red marked the porch corners. I see Ceredo and Kate's big house more clearly from my family's stories than I do from my early childhood memories of visits there. And I can hear the busy buzzing of the hummingbirds that clustered around the hollyhocks, for each of us planted them in our gardens—then forever fought to control the far-reaching seedlings—because that's what our mothers did.

According to my grandmother's stories, the best part of growing up was summer evenings in Ceredo. That was when neighbors gathered on the swings and steps and in the cushioned chairs on those spacious porches. There the young people talked and laughed, courting really, while the West Virginia sunlight slowly faded. As the mist rose from the Ohio and Big Sandy rivers and edged inland in almost imperceptible increments, the porches turned into concealed worlds, rooms with walls of softly shifting fleece. Then, when a foghorn from a river barge struck a muffled chord, someone would begin to sing: We were sailin' along on Moonlight Bay . . .

No porch was as popular as Frank and Kate's. Theirs was a family of musicians. Each of the children was skilled in piano and voice. With pride the family spoke of Glen Ford's tours around the States with the University of Colorado Glee Club during his college and law school years—tours that Kate tracked from picture postcards she faithfully kept, as did my grandmother and mother and as I do now. Lena too had a clear, vibrant voice and dreamed of musical theater as a career. On these evenings Wynemah—who already was playing Scott Joplin's complicated rags and like all of us could "play most anything by ear"—was the designated accompanist. So on summer nights the heavy rosewood piano was shouldered onto the porch through the wide front door; Glen Ford would grab his mandolin and guitar, my grandmother would push the ornate round piano stool with the red velvet, tufted seat up to the piano, and the Mott children and their friends would sing.

When visitors stepped from the shadowed front porch with the graceful white columns into Kate's spacious front hall, they were struck by the ornate staircase leading to the floors above and by the gleaming brass chandelier hanging from the sky blue ceiling high overhead. It was Frank's idea that all the ceilings in the house should be painted blue as a joyful reminder of heaven—this perhaps because of his fateful talk with God during the drought. The richness of those ceilings reflected the sumptuousness of the rooms throughout the house—rooms filled with furniture that Frank shipped up the Ohio River from Cincinnati to his "black-eyed baby."

The rooms in "the elegant gem" were large. Kizzie Clay's couch, gracefully framed by a wide ogee-curved band of mahogany across the back, was in the sitting room. Its black velvet upholstery—the choice of covering for Kate's generation—looked stately against the deep red background of the flowered body Brussels wall-to-wall carpet that covered the main rooms in the downstairs and climbed up the wide stairs to the bedrooms above. In the dining room was a chestnut gate-legged table with enough additional leaves to accommodate the growing family. The backs of the cushioned chairs were carved with flowers formed from a multitude of petals. A matching mirrored sideboard stood against the long wall next to the swinging butler's door to the kitchen.

The natural wood shutters in each room were kept closed during the day with louvers slanted to catch the air but deflect the rays of the sun. Shadows filled the corners and further darkened the walnut, mahogany, and cherry of the furniture—light woods, with the exception of an occasional tiger maple piece, were considered by the family to be of lower quality. Still, in most rooms there were pools of light from kerosene reading lamps set on marble-topped tables beside comfortable chairs. Reading was Kate's greatest pleasure, and, as with the music, she had raised a family of readers.

In the corner of the sitting room near Kizzie's couch was a bookshelf with heavy glass doors. Inside were leather volumes on diverse subjects: Stoddard's *Lectures*; books on beekeeping; Collins's *History of Kentucky,* which chronicled John Mavity Burns's political career; a copy of Ely's *History of the Big Sandy Valley,* which also included the Burns family and a picture of Kate's father; and—my mother's favorite—*Dr. Chase's Recipes or Information for Everybody* published in Ann Arbor in the 1840s.

Dr. Chase's Recipes is the one acknowledgment I have that Kizzie Clay related in some way to her daughter Kate. The book was originally Kizzie's, and, as the story goes, she gave it to Kate when she married James Ward. From Kate it went to her Ida Lee, then to Lena, the second sister, and on to Wynemah, the baby. Next *Dr. Chase's Recipes* came to Mother, who sat for hours reading it as a child when she visited her grandmother. Now it is mine. The pages are frayed and foxed. The frontispiece is gone. One of the Cecil mothers has penciled a remedy for the treatment of measles on the inside of the front cover, and another mother—if my former medieval skill of hand differentiation is still intact—has done some quick financial calculations on the inside back cover. A small envelope with "How to Make Violet Beads" inscribed on the front in Lena's hand has a newspaper recipe tucked inside. A brown newspaper obituary for Ida Lee's husband, Charles Thomas Bishop, flakes between pages 220 and 221.

Upstairs in the "elegant gem" were the bedrooms for the children, with extras for guests. Above those were rooms for the help. The girls shared rooms. Glen Ford had his own. Most important of all was Kate and Frank's bedroom. There was a cherry bedstead carved with water lilies and a matching large dresser and smaller washstand, each topped with elegant pink marble. The room stretched across the front of the house and was large enough to have a sitting room with a view of the yard and the church across the street. This was Kate's favorite room. She came here to read or to simply gaze out the window. Eventually she came here to hide.

Frank's heavenly blue ceilings may have lightened the dark opulence in the house. They did not lighten the dark spirits in the family. Kate did not like to mother her children nor did she enjoy being around them. When the children were small she had constant help, and Frank was always there to nurture his "Dear Little Dolly Dumpling Lena" or his "Little Indian Wynemah." When the children were older—and Ida Lee, who was hard to handle, was out of the house—Kate thought the children should take care of themselves. Yet they still made demands on her, demands that Kate had no interest in meeting. So Kate did something that has haunted each Cecil mother since. She repaired to her room.

One bright early autumn afternoon, Kate Burns Mott walked up the handsome, wide front stairs that Frank had built, past the chandelier hanging from the heavenly blue ceiling, went into her bedroom, closed the door, and stayed. She had given no indication to her husband or her children that she intended to withdraw from the family. It was 1897, and she was fifty-three years old. Her mother, Kizzie, had died the year before. Her father, John, was happily married to Ole Jose. Her husband, Frank, was a frail sixty-nine. Lena, the oldest child at home, was twenty-one and on her way to join her sister Lee in New York. Glen, the Crown Prince, was fourteen, and Wynemah, the baby, was only eleven.

First Lena, and later Wynemah, did Kate's laundry, cleaned the kerosene lamps, emptied the chamber pot, and kept her in food, library books, newspapers, bourbon, and wine. The children knew that their mother was selfish and that she had been spoiled by their grandfather and then by their father. They knew she was not interested in her children—except perhaps for Glen, though even that was now in question. Still, they were unprepared for such an extreme act. To make matters worse, they did not know if Kate would ever rejoin the family.

Kate spent a year upstairs, refusing all entreaties from Frank or the children to leave her room. That year marks a turning point in the family. Before Kate walked up those ornate front stairs, the Clay and Cecil mothers had managed to raise and educate their children with a certain amount of grace and a lot of help. They may not have liked mothering, they may not have been nurturers, but they had nursemaids whom they could hand their children to. Also, each woman had chosen a mate who would be both mother and father to their children.

When Kate withdrew from her family she offered a treacherous option to all of the family's future mothers: if you have had enough, you can always just "go upstairs." From that fall in 1897 on, each of us had to fight that temptation. And sometimes we lost.

One year after Kate walked upstairs, she walked back down the front stairs into the wide front hall with the blue ceiling. Her return to the dark elegance of the downstairs was as unexpected as her departure. Frank Mott welcomed her back as if nothing had happened. In fact, as the story was told in the family, nothing had happened. There was never an indication that Kate's behavior was unusual. The year upstairs was simply one of Kate's stories.

I did confront Mother once about my great-grandmother's year upstairs. Mother suspected that I was planning to see a therapist, and she forbade me to go. "I will not have it!" said Mother. "No one in our family has ever had mental disorders!" "What about Kate, Mother?" I asked. "What about the year she spent upstairs? Wasn't that a mental breakdown?" "That was not a mental breakdown! That was nervous prostration." And that was the abrupt end of the discussion. The tale of Kate's year upstairs was never recounted again in my presence.

Kate's year upstairs did not soften her outlook on life. She continued to complain bitterly about her trials, that "no one appreciates me"—a phrase I know well since it was one of my grandmother's refrains. A letter that Frank wrote to Lena best describes the mood of the household a few years after Kate came back downstairs.

Ceredo, WVa November 5, 1907 Friday

To My Dear Little Dolly Dumpling Lena

Your Ma got a letter from you this morning but as she hardly ever says anything about her letters I must ask her so she keeps it to herself. Well your Sister Ida Lee Bishop is here and enjoying herself quite much. It is not necessary to say anything about her. I am about as usual. Nothing to do so am as well contented as could be under the circumstances. Glen is here. I think he is improving as fast as could be under the circumstances. The old lady is going about with a rag around her head with headache. She says she has too much hard work to do that she can't stand so much hard work. I help her all I can and still she thinks her job is the hardest of all people living. So I guess it is. Little Indian will be sick in a week or so [Wynemah was about to have a baby] and after that I am going away for a spell. She has the hardest time of any other woman in the world. She has everything to make her happy and she ought to be contented but she is not. So I let her go and have her own way about it. Well I hope you are well and having a fair share of happiness. Well treat yourself with sunshine and that will keep off the blues. So I will quit. Wishing you all the happy sunshine in the world from your father Frank Mott.

Dwight Hawkins "Frank" Mott died on February 24, 1912, four years after that letter was written. He was eighty-two. Mother adored her grandfather with the curly silver gray hair and smiling brown eyes. Her favorite memories of him were sitting in his lap and leaning into the warmth of his chest while he rocked and sang to her in a sweet tenor voice. When she described the way his breath smelled of whiskey—the rock and rye he usually had near him—she would have a faraway look and a slow smile that barely touched the corners of her mouth. I did not like that look of Mother's. I always wondered if that final sip of rye and the rock candy that he gave her from the bottom of his whisky glass precipitated her love affair with alcohol.

Kate outlived Frank by twenty-two years. She, unlike her husband, did not age well. John Burns, Kate's father, had described this period of "wilt" and "wither" to his much-loved Kate in a message he wrote in her keepsake album more than fifty years before her death. It is dated August 26, 1861, and Kate had just turned seventeen.

My Kate, it is almost autumn and all nature is in the yellow leaf of decay. The leaves of the flowers that so lately blushed upon their stems are one by one falling reminding us that all things earthly must wilt, wither, and perish. You Miss Kate are in the morning of life with all its rich fragrance and beauty around you. Your young and innocent heart as yet has felt none of the keen pangs of grief but ere the autumn of life overtakes you those large beautiful black eyes will be suffused with many a tear and your young frame will heave with a many a sigh and like the flowers my Kate you too must fade.

The roses of beauty that now blush upon your young beautiful and sinless cheek must wither and die in the decay of age. You my Kate are the rival of all the flowers in beauty but like myself Miss Kate when autumn's blast shall have faded thy young face and wrinkles affix where roses now bloom and blush you will realize the fact that there is nothing true but Heaven. JMB

Catharine Rebecca "Kate" Burns Mott died in "the elegant gem" on February 11, 1934, in the spacious, sunny bedroom with the chair by the window that looked out on the Congregational Church across the street. Her death came from a brief bout of pneumonia. She was five months short of her ninetieth birthday. Two of her granddaughters—children of Louisa Ward, her oldest child, whom she had cut out of her will two years before—tried to pull the phlegm from their grandmother's throat while Wynemah cried hysterically in the corner of Kate's favorite room.

The Crown Prince—mayor of Ceredo at the time of Kate's death—inherited the house. Mother was twenty-seven when Kate died, and she mourned the loss of her grandmother. Kate, it seems, was—like many of the Cecil mothers—a better grandmother than she was a mother. Mother refused to look at Kate in the casket and cried for months after her death. Louisa Ward, maligned by her mother despite her sweet and gentle nature, remained the much loved "Sister Lou" who provided a comforting base in later life for family visits. Kate's three Mott daughters were not so forgiving of their mother's self-centered behavior and her favoritism toward their brother Glen. But then those three—Lee, Lena, and Wynemah—had always been a force to be reckoned with.

9

Strong Women

ONE EVENING when I was eleven Mother turned to me while she, my grandmother Wynemah, and I were doing the dinner dishes and said, "You are from a long line of strong women and you will be strong like all the rest. You know your Aunt Lena once had a syphilitic sore on her upper lip. She got syphilis from the man she had an affair with when she lived in New York with her sister Lee. When she had the sore removed, Lee walked straight into the operating room to make sure Lena's beauty would not be destroyed. Lena was more beautiful after the surgery than she was before."

It was late summer the first time the Strong Women story was told to me. Lena had recently died, and my grandmother and my mother were still grieving. We were in Wynemah's kitchen. She was at the sink washing the supper dishes. Mother was drying and handing plates and glasses to me to put away. The last of the day's sunlight raced across the deep ravine outside the window, streaked across the kitchen, and landed in the tall pedestal bowl of red glass fairy balls on the banquet table in the dining room. As the story unfolded, the glass balls captured the golden evening light and threw it back toward me in waves of hot ember red, a pulsing scarlet fire that in my adolescent mind's eye inflamed the sore on Aunt Lena's soft, delicate lips. At age eleven I did not know what a syphilitic sore was, but I did know that beauty was prized in the family.

My grandmother Wynemah and her sisters, Lee and Lena, were noted for their dark, striking features—features passed down from their grandfather John Mavity Burns. John Burns had a face of perfect proportions. In his pictures his dark eyes, framed by smoothly curved brows and broad, sculptured cheek- bones, look tranquilly toward the lens, confident that the camera will disclose no flaws. He had brown curly hair, a chiseled nose, and full sensuous lips. Although his daughter Kate looked little like her father, the loveliness of Kate's three daughters reverted back to John—and to his grandmother, Elizabeth Roland Burns, who was noted in a usually prim nineteenth-century history of the Big Sandy River valley as "a brunette of a most perfect type; hair as black as a raven, heavy eye-brows, a curved lip, and a fault- less figure."

The sisters, Lee, Lena, and Wynemah Mott, each had masses of brown curly hair and brown eyes so saturated they appeared black. Their coloring was richer and their cheekbones were more prominent than John Burns's—a reflection of their father's dark, handsome features that came in part from his modicum of Indian blood. Yet they definitely resembled their grandfather.

Lee, the oldest of the three sisters, was said to be striking, but there are few pictures of her and none that clearly shows her face. Lena, the second sister and "the angel" in the family, was well documented. She was tall and willowy. There was a Gibson Girl look about her, with her long, lush hair pulled up and back in that popular look of the late nineteenth century. When she smiled, which she did often, her eyes lit up and a dimple flickered near the left side of her mouth. Lena complained of her long nose, which came from the Clay side of the family and mirrored her cousin Henry Clay's, yet she had a cupid-bow upper lip that had been enhanced by the removal of the syphilitic sore.

Of the three sisters, the youngest, Wynemah, looked most like her grandfather and was the most beautiful. Her face was shaped like his, as was her nose and her full lower lip. Her eyes, however, were her own. They were black, more pronounced than his. Her thick, wavy black hair was tinged with natural henna highlights. She was of medium height with a figure of perfect proportions for her day. Yet it was not her figure, nor her confident, chin-lifted carriage, that was so compelling. It was the way she looked out of her eyes. Rather than having John Burns's clear, open gaze, Wynemah had the sultry look of a temptress even at a young age. There was something startling about her dark beauty, an aura of the exotic that was breathtaking. Throughout her life men stopped and stared as Wynemah self-assuredly strolled down the street—tales of men stopping in mid-stride as she walked by were some of her favorite stories.

It was Mother who told the Strong Women story that first time, standing at the sink beside her mother, but it was Wynemah who repeated Lena's unfortunate plight and miraculous rescue to me, her impressionable granddaughter, numerous times during the next thirteen years. After Wynemah died, Mother continued with the theme. The words were mantra-like in their sameness: "You are from a long line of strong women, and you will be strong like all the rest. You know Aunt Lena once had a syphilitic sore . . ."

I never forgot the Strong Women story despite my attempts to flee the family mold. It floated near the inner banks of my psyche into my adult life and still resides there. I have often wondered why this particular story about my sweet, dear Great-Aunt Lena—whom I had lived with for several weeks and who had so many more flattering stories—was the one I most remembered. I now think I know why. I remembered that particular story because it set down a formula; it provided a structural format for a type of story that was told not just about Lena but also about other women in the family. I did not think of it this way when I was younger, but then, in my late thirties, when I was teaching at the School of the Art Institute of Chicago, I added a new course to the ones I was regularly teaching on classical and medieval art history. The course was on mythology and symbolism—topics I had studied for years—but instead of covering only myths, I decided to include a few lectures on fairy tales. That was when I began to realize that the repeated recitation of the Strong Women story quite possibly had a purpose—or at least an effect.

Myths serve a distinct function. They attempt to explain the inexplicable—creation, death, rebirth—and to set down rules regarding social behaviors—incest, patricide, matricide. Myths provide a structure to understand life's great questions, and the themes in myths are the same whether one is born in the steamy rainforests of South America, on the great rolling plains of North America, or in the lush river valleys of Mesopotamia. Fairy tales serve the same purpose. They give children a point of comparison for their fears of abandonment, their feelings of jealousy, their angers. Further, they provide a road map—like Hansel and Gretel's bread crumbs—to find a way through the frightening forest of young life.

So there I was, teaching about the function of myths and fairy tales throughout history, when one night, just before I fell fully asleep, I heard my grandmother's voice telling me, "You are from a long line of strong women and you will be strong like all the rest. You know Aunt Lena once had a syphilitic sore on her upper lip. She got syphilis from the man she had an affair with when she lived in New York with her sister Lee. When she had the sore removed, Lee walked straight into the operating room to make sure Lena's beauty would not be destroyed. Lena was more beautiful after the surgery than she was before."

This time I listened, really listened, from beginning to end, and finally I began to realize that the Strong Women story was told to me over and over for a reason. As in myths and fairy tales, the story seemed to relay a message my mother and grandmother thought was important for me to know—a message about sex coupled with strength. The story's structure goes like this: furtive sex plus public exposure plus family intervention equal female strength. But how could this be, and why would Mother and Wynemah think this information was important for me to know when at first telling I was not old enough to be sexually active and had no idea what syphilis was? Then I remembered that I had started menstruating when I was eleven, just a few months before the story's first telling.

Alright, I thought. I see why I was told the Strong Women story when I was, but how does sex convert to strength? Where is the connection there? Then I remembered Wynemah's stories about men stopping mid-step to stare at her when she was eighteen, twenty, thirty, forty—men left speechless when she walked by, men losing all sense of decorum. Wynemah greatly valued this power she wielded over men and loved to tell the Men Stopping on the Street stories. It was this sense of power, I believe, this ability to control men through her sultry, sensual beauty that caused Wynemah—and then Mother—to equate strength with sex, to connect strength to her beloved and beautiful sister Lena's sexual escapade.

I now believe that when Wynemah and Mother told the Strong Women story they were confirming for themselves and for me—the only girl in my generation—that the women in the family were sexual creatures. They were also informing me that our sexuality sometimes fell outside the norms of propriety. At the same time they were assuring me that if our sexual excursions became known in a potentially embarrassing way, the family would protect us. Both mothers, in effect, were giving me permission to be sexual outside of marriage, to "be strong like all the rest." I did not get the message on a conscious level until I was in my late thirties. I did, however, get it subconsciously much, much earlier.

On thinking back I realized that another member of the family had lived out the family formula before Lena's stay in New York—Wynemah's sister Ida Lee. Ida Lee Mott was born in 1872, Kate and Frank Mott's first child. She was four years older than her sister Lena and fourteen years older than my grandmother Wynemah. Lee was considered willful and short-tempered. In fact, she was almost always angry at something or somebody, and that somebody was often her baby sister Wynemah. One story goes that when young Lee discovered that Wynemah had wandered into her bedroom and crawled onto her bed—something Lee had told her never to do—Lee went into a fury and determined to dump Wynemah down the well. Kate, their mother, who had yet to repair upstairs, was reading in her bedroom when she first heard the screams—two sets coming from the back of the house. One sounded like seething fury, the other was saturated with utter fear. She put down her book and went down the back stairs to investigate. It was good she did, for Kate reached the kitchen door just in time to seize Wynemah's feet as Lee dragged her by her hair headfirst down the back-porch stairs.

Wynemah later stressed how strong she had been the day Sister Lee tried to kill her. She hung onto the porch railing with all her baby strength while she screamed for her mother. She hung on and on as Lee dragged her down those rough wooden steps by her long, thick hair, screaming her intent to drop her down the well. "It is a wonder I have any hair left at all," Wynemah told me. It seems Lee did not let go when Kate grabbed Wynemah's feet. For a few horrifying moments Wynemah's tiny toddler body was a writhing, twisted rope in a tug of war between mother and daughter, the irate mother who clung to her feet and the anger-possessed teenage daughter who would not let go of the grip she had on Baby Wynemah's hair.

My grandmother learned to stay out of her sister's way after that. In fact, the entire family stayed out of Lee's way, including Kate, who basically washed her hands of her daughter. Ida Lee was mean. The family agreed on that point.

Since no one talked much about "Sister Lee," I did not learn another story about her until some years after the Strong Women story. Around 1890, when she was still a teenager, Lee got pregnant. The partner was thought to be either a local sweetheart or a beau from Louisa, Kentucky, where she frequently visited cousins. Lee would never disclose which of the two young men the potential father was—perhaps she did not know. As soon as the pregnancy was revealed, the family put Lee on a train headed for Chicago to have an abortion.

There was never an elaboration of the trip. Did someone travel with her—her mother perhaps, or an older half-sister from her father's first marriage? Why Chicago and where did she stay? There was family there. One of Frank's older daughters from his first marriage—the three beauties' half-sister—had married a Wurlitzer in Chicago. She could have been trusted with knowledge of Lee's unfortunate situation. But none of this information was ever disclosed.

Lee's story, however, did not end here. There is still the formulaic happy ending, the part of the equation in the Strong Women narrative where family intervention after a sexual mishap makes life better than it was before, and the miscreant becomes "strong like all the rest."

Lee did not return home after the abortion. Rather, her parents sent her to Maryland Teachers' College in Baltimore. After teachers' college Lee decided that she wanted to be a nurse, so Kate and Frank Mott paid for their daughter's nursing training in New York City. Kate wanted little to do with Lee, and the longer she was in school, the longer she was out of the house. Plus there was always the possibility that she might meet someone in Maryland or New York—or anywhere but home—and decide to stay. Which in fact she did. For Ida Lee Mott the happy ending of the Strong Women story came when she met Charles Bishop.

Charles Thomas Bishop was Lee's first patient after nursing training. He was recovering from an appendectomy, and Lee Mott had been assigned to be his private nurse. Charles, or Uncle Charley as the family called him, fell deeply in love with his beautiful, dark-eyed nurse and soon proposed. At the time of their heady romance and marriage Charles Bishop was the Paymaster of the U.S. Navy in New York. He came from a wealthy Philadelphia family—the son of Stillwell Shaw Bishop, who had founded a line of clipper ships that sailed out of Philadelphia. Although it was usual for the mothers in my family to think that their daughters had married "beneath themselves," Kate was happy about Lee's choice of a husband. The family's only concern was that "poor, sweet Charley" might not be strong enough to hold his own against mean, manipulative, ill-tempered Lee.

Still, Lee and Charles Bishop seemed to be a happy couple. I know this because I have Lee's *Happenings in Our Home* journal started on December 7, 1903—her wedding day. In the journal she describes trips from New York to Philadelphia, to Detroit, to Niagara Falls, to the Cape. On their first wedding anniversary Charles gave Lee "Thackeray's 14 volumes" and on her birthday a diamond ring. They continued to travel extensively and party extravagantly, and eventually they settled in Boston. There were, however, no children. It seems that Lee and Charles wanted them, especially Uncle Charley, as the story went, but they were unable to conceive. The suspicion in the family was that the abortion not only caused the loss of one child but also any future children. I always wondered, but never learned, if Charles Bishop knew why he never became a father.

Lee Mott Bishop rarely returned home for visits. Still, she stayed in touch with the family. In her *Happenings* journal, she writes about the weddings of her sisters, Lena and Wynemah— only two weeks apart in October 1905—and pastes in newspaper clippings of each event. Mother's birth is recorded, and Lena's husband's obituary is tucked between the pages of the book, as is that of her own husband, Charles Bishop.

After Uncle Charley's death in 1920, the fairytale ending of Lee's story is over. Although she was left with money, she returned to nursing and became the supervisor of a children's wing in a Boston hospital. Lee was addicted to alcohol, and easy access to drugs on her hospital ward added to the problem. Eventually Lee resigned from her nursing position to work with her addictions, yet, sadly, she was never able to fully overcome them. By this time she had married Albert Walter, a widower who stayed with her—despite her personality and her addictions—until she died in her late sixties. The telling last line of the addendum to Ida Lee Mott's Strong Women story was actually about Albert Walter. His sister-in-law Lena, who rarely said anything bad about anyone, described him as "a nice guy until he married Ida Lee."

After I stepped back from the Strong Women story and examined its structure and underlying meaning, I began to wonder what messages might inhabit other segments of the Clay-Cecil oral history. It was evident that when Rebecca Cecil married William Clay and became the keeper of the family's stories, the story lines changed. Hero stories were no longer in vogue. Goddess stories rose to the fore. And with the dark tales of the Cecil mothers a new narrative emerged, one about mothers and sons, about boy-children protected by their mothers.

Mother-son narratives have been recounted for millennia. In every culture—Mesopotamia, Greece, Rome, Native America—the structure is the same. A goddess procreates with a mortal man and bears a son. The son, though half mortal, is empowered by his mother's divine bloodline and is able to accomplish wondrous feats. This story line—the "divine kingship" myth—starts showing up in our family with Kate Burns Mott and her son, Glen. Glen's sisters were unusually prescient when they named their brother "the Crown Prince."

Glen Ford Mott was his mother's only living son and her favorite. He was designated from birth to be the lawyer and legislator who would follow in the footsteps of Kate's beloved father, John Mavity Burns. Glen dutifully served as a page in the West Virginia legislature in Charleston and later attended the University of Colorado, studying law, singing and touring his way through school. When he graduated he studied for the bar. Having passed the examination, according to a family anecdote, he made a one-sentence statement in response to the congratulations of the presiding judge: "This is the first and the last time I will ever stand before the bench." With that, he quit the law and talked his mother into supporting him for a year at the University of Vermont—this time to study agriculture and journalism, his real loves.

According to his sisters, Glen was a handsome, debonair gadfly, always optimistic. He flitted around the country, traveled on a cargo ship through the Panama Canal, lived in New York, proofread for Theodore Dreiser, purchased a vineyard near Modesta with his wife, Ethel Trimble—almost all adventures supported by Kate's inheritance from her father. Although each venture failed, and he and Ethel lost their only child, Dwight Hawkins Mott, Glen always pulled through. Mother remembers her uncle as happy and expectant each day with the thought that a letter would arrive from a publisher to say that a short story or a novel that was making the rounds had been accepted.

After the loss of their son and their vineyard, Glen and Ethel returned to Ceredo to live with Kate in "the elegant gem." Although Kate never really accepted Ethel—even the Crown Prince had married beneath himself—Glen was happy. He farmed, he was elected mayor of Ceredo, and in 1941 his second novel, *Push Boat,* was published. Glen Ford Mott was a local success. His mother, had she been alive, would have been proud, but then she always knew he had good genes. He carried the Cecil blood.

10

LITTLE DOLLY DUMPLING

HE SECOND of Kate and Frank's daughters was the angel of
the family. Lena Leota Mott was born on August 19, 1876.
Everyone loved Lena. She was the only daughter of Kate and
Frank's who was unruffled and sweet-natured. Even the Rebel
neighbor next door would chat with her despite the running feud
he and Frank had over the war. It was probably because of her
natural sweetness and even temper that Lena got away with flout-
ing community mores throughout her life. That and her poise.

Lena was described by the family as following in the Cecil
footsteps. She had an aristocratic carriage, innate sophistication,
and impeccable taste. Lena's dream was to sing professionally.
First she had to gain the emotional strength to wrench herself
away from her demanding mother—who was still in her room
upstairs—and to leave Wynemah and their aging father. According to family lore, Ida Lee had no qualms about urging Lena to
leave Ceredo, and finally Lena joined her older sister in New
York. Soon after the affair with her syphilitic lover, Lena left

New York to study voice at the Boston Conservatory of Music. Yet after a year of study her life changed. Lena was diagnosed with tuberculosis and was forced to give up her dream of performance. She started over.

While still living at home, Lena—like Wynemah later—took a year of business training at Marshall College in Huntington, West Virginia. Consequently, after her training at the Boston Conservatory ended, Lena took a job as a secretary in the Wood's Paint Factory in Wellesley, Massachusetts. The syphilitic scar had added the cupid's bow to Lena's lips. Henry Wood Junior, the owner's son and a friend of Lee's new husband, Charles Bishop, took one look at Lena and fell in love.

I can picture "Uncle Harry" Wood only as an elderly man and as a young boy. The former is from two portraits that hung in heavy gilt frames over the fireplaces in our living room—portraits not of Harry but of his father and his mother. The latter is from a portrait of Harry himself as a young boy with a mop of brown curly hair. Years ago I inherited this small, delicately detailed oil painting of the young Harry and his two elegantly dressed sisters—Frances and Mame—painted in the third quarter of the nineteenth century. The three children are positioned on a bed of grass that appears to be sprinkled with roses. A closer look shows that they are framed by a bush of their father's famous hybrid rose: the Waban Rose, named for the lake that edged their estate in Wellesley, Massachusetts.

Young Harry stands between the girls, dressed in a high-buttoned dark blue jacket and short pants trimmed in blue braid and white lace. Around his neck is a fringed satin scarf in the softest of blues. One of his sisters reaches toward her young brother. She has a toy soldier in her hand that she has taken from a wooden chest at Harry's feet. But Harry stares straight ahead because this portrait is about him. He is his father's only son and heir to the family business and estate, the Crown Prince of the Wood family.

The Henry Wood's Sons Company Paint Factory—"Maker of Fine Colors"—was founded in 1837 and located on the western edge of Wellesley College. Harry's father, George Henry Wood Senior, ran the family enterprise during the day and was a horticulturist and philanderer by night. Harry Junior was a popular Harvard graduate—an alumnus of the Hasty Pudding Club— and owner of a string of prizewinning trotting horses. Although Harry was a few years older than Lena and already a widower, Lena married Harry Wood in October 1905 in the Little Church around the Corner in New York. She was twenty-nine. The family always suspected that Harry's money and his beautiful estate, Wellesley, had a lot to do with Lena's decision to marry him. Whatever the reason, Wellesley became Wynemah and Mother's summer home. For Mother, especially, it was a fairyland that framed her life's desires from childhood on.

Wellesley was the stage set for Mother's childhood. It was there in the small lake on the property—Lake Waban—that she learned to swim, there she learned to ride—on one of the tamer ponies in Uncle Harry's several stables, there she was allowed to pick a bouquet of fresh roses every day from the family's famous greenhouses. And it was there she felt safe from her mother's unpredictable anger, for Wynemah was happy when she was with her favorite sister Lena. Even if Wynemah lost her temper, Mother knew "Auntie" would protect her, for Katie Carrie—as Mother was called then—was the closest thing to her own child Lena would ever have.

Wellesley was a magic place that I see clearly through the stories—more clearly than I do from the snapshots I have of my toddler mother sitting on the wide steps of the deep-shadowed porch, more clearly than the pictures of the two beautiful sisters laughing into the lens. I see the spacious grounds at Wellesley in the summer and the fall. I see the giant trees and the stables, and I see Lake Waban encircled by rich red Massachusetts maples. I know well the greenhouses where Harry's father developed the Waban Rose, and I see the brilliant blue hydrangea hedges that bank both sides of the long curving drive leading to the house.

I am glad that I can see Wellesley through Mother's eyes, because the reality of Harry and Lena's estate today is harsh. I always knew that the Wood family had given land early on to Wellesley College, which sided their property to the east. I also knew that Harry's sisters Frances and Mame had gotten their degrees there. I did not know until I delved into Wellesley College's archives that in 1932 the college bought the Wood family's entire estate—paint factory, ponds, all. Nor did I know before I began to corroborate Mother's stories about her summers at Wellesley what danger little Katie Carrie was in when she splashed and played in the waters of Lake Waban.

The college archives show that the Henry Wood's Paint Factory was a massive operation that spread out over approximately six acres of land. The main house was at the end of a long drive. Behind the house were Harry Senior's greenhouses for his roses and the stables for Harry Junior's trotting horses. Farther on— and well out of sight of the main house and grounds—was a large house for the "Foreman of the Works," a rooming house for out-of-town workers, a tall freestanding smokestack, and numerous brick factory buildings that at the factory's peak produced daily nearly six tons of dry pigment to be mixed by purchasers into paint. A train spur ran through the center of the clustered factory buildings, as did a brook—Trail Race—and toward the edge of the factory site was Paintshop Pond.

The usual method of producing pigments for paint in the nineteenth century was to wash minerals with a natural water source and deposit the waste products nearby. The Wood's Paint Factory site was well chosen. Pigments made from lead chromates, lead sulfates, and lead nitrates were washed with the water of Trail Race. Wastes were dumped into Paintshop Pond. Mother's summertime dreamland—like all the water sources in a wide surrounding area including Lake Waban and eventually the Charles River—was contaminated with lead and chromium and other mineral wastes produced by Henry Wood's Paint Factory.

At first it was difficult for me to separate Mother's stories about her peaceful, play-filled summers at Wellesley from the dreary scientific accounts of the contaminated property Wellesley College purchased in 1932. Yet the college's archived maps and descriptions of the property gave me the opportunity to examine Wellesley from an aerial view rather than from the ground view one gets from photographs, or the visual descriptions of a short-legged child. So, as I examined an overview of the site and found the long drive that ran up to the multi-turreted roof of the main house, I was swept into one of Lena's stories. This time, as I remembered the incident, I could literally see where the story took place.

Lena is in a carriage coming up the drive toward the house. The trotting horse she chose that day for her shopping in Wellesley Center is the most spirited in Harry's stable. Later the family angrily asks the head groom, Jordan, why he allowed Lena—six months pregnant—to take out this particular stallion. From the story and the archived bird's-eye view I watch the prancing horse. Something is wrong. The horse shies—no one knows what spooked it. Lena is an excellent horsewoman but she cannot rein the horse in. She loses control. The carriage flips over and Lena is thrown across the fluff-balls of blue hydrangeas onto the ground beyond the drive. She loses the baby and never gets pregnant again. From the photos I see the long drive to the house where Lena's accident occurred. Her story takes on a reality for me that it never did before.

I loved Lena Leota Mott Wood. I loved her because Wynemah and Mother loved her, and I loved her because, even when I was young, I recognized something special about her—her evocative choice of words, the fascinating paintings she made and the unusual clothes she wore, her calm modulated voice, her sweetness. I wanted to be like her. But most of all I loved my glamorous great-aunt because she shamelessly smoked violet-scented cigarettes "on the street."

I relished the stories about Lena's visits home in the first decade of the twentieth century. I could see Lena as she ambled along the sidewalks of small-town Ceredo in her stylish Bergdorf clothes. She was tall and lithe and had those dark eyes we all have and that lush mahogany hair. She was bedecked in jewels and furs. Her diamond rings flashed in the sunlight each time she languidly raised the cigarette to her lips. No well-bred lady smoked in public, no lady did such a thing, the neighbors whispered as she glided by with cigarette in hand. But then she is a Mott, and a Burns, and a Cecil, and a Clay; maybe ladies smoke on the street in Boston and New York.

From the first moment I heard the violet-scented cigarettes story, I chose Lena as my role model. I knew she had a quiet, gentle nature, but now I also knew she had a mischievous, devilish spirit. She carried herself with poise, as I was already being trained to do, and she had used that poise to walk self-assuredly through her hometown's local mores. She was herself—despite the family's undertow. Further, no storyteller said that Lena in her boldness ever "let the family down." At night as I was growing up I would sometimes lie in bed thinking about the cigarettes. In my imagination those cigarettes that belonged to my magnificent, worldly great-aunt were not only scented with violets, they were lavender in color. I saw delicate lavender cylinders of the subtlest tint that looked lovely against Lena's lightly rouged syphilitic-scarred lip. And I would smile to myself about Lena's roguish daring as I drifted off.

Lena followed in her grandmother Kizzie Clay's footsteps. Like Kizzie, she chose to divorce an adulterous husband. In fact, she divorced him twice. Harry inherited both money and lifestyle from his father. Henry Senior had been an avid horticulturist who spent as much time as possible in his greenhouses hybridizing roses. According to the family, Henry Senior had several mistresses. Every day he sent a dozen roses from his gardens to each mistress and a final dozen to his wife.

Harry Junior, like his father, found it normal to philander, and after a number of his painful affairs Lena divorced him. He won her back after a short period, however, and to commemorate their second engagement he gave Lena a flawless three-stone diamond ring and a five-diamond wedding band from Tiffany's. Mother inherited the rings. They belong to me now, and as they pass from mother to daughter in the family they will continue to be described as they have always been: "Aunt Lena's engagement and wedding rings from the second time she married Uncle Harry Wood."

Sadly, Harry's philandering did not stop after the second marriage, and Lena crept back to Ceredo one summer to recuperate from a second divorce and a double mastectomy. I have a poignant reminder of that period in her life—a rectangular wooden trunk with low sides and a flat-hinged lid. The trunk, loosely sheathed in stained, shredded remnants of grass cloth, is filled with mementoes from Lena's life—favorite linens and photographs that Lena chose to tuck away.

I think for each of us who inherited Lena's memories—Wynemah, Mother, and me—the physicality of the trunk itself reminded us of Lena. The hint of the exotic in the grass cloth and the bamboo trim symbolized her travels, her lifestyle, her taste. We all knew that the contents were also about Lena, but after the first perusal no one needed again to look inside. The existence of the trunk was enough. I must have remembered on an unconscious level, however, what lay within Lena's trunk. For on a day when I was doggedly packing for a move I did not want to make I impetuously sat down on the floor in front of that rectangle box with its ragged dusty sheathing and laid back the lid.

Inside, wrapped in tissue paper and in perfect condition, were tablecloths in white linen and off-white damask and one in a delicate creamy yellow tastefully embroidered with clusters of grapes and leaves in the same soft color of silk thread. There were dozens of handkerchief-linen napkins with hand-hemmed edges that had squares of Belgian lace carefully sown into a corner. There were blue ribbons from Harry's trotting-horse days and pictures of the horses and Wellesley and the grounds. There were pictures of Mother and Wynemah and Lena and laughter and good times.

Near the bottom of the trunk, under the pictures and ribbons, was another tissue-wrapped package. This one was not heavy like the others, but soft and feather-light. Gingerly I removed the paper. Inside were numerous handmade camisoles. Some were peach silk, and others were made from delicate handkerchief linen. All were sewn with tiny, evenly spaced stitches that showed the patience and skill of the seamstress. They were elegant and lovely—just like Lena. Then, as I held up one camisole after another, I noticed something peculiar about the shape. When I realized what it was, I started to cry. The camisoles were tailored to fit tight against my beautiful, graceful Aunt Lena's flattened chest after her breast cancer surgery. Where the breasts should have been were delicate handmade lace pockets. The pockets had a slight fullness to them—just enough to put in padding to fill out a tall, still lithe, Gibson-girl figure.

I could not bear to keep the camisoles with their tiny pockets where I would see them often, so they are still in the shredded grass cloth–covered trunk underneath the blue ribbons and the photographs. I store the trunk under the high four-poster cherry bed that was my grandmother's before it came to me. I figure the sisters can be together that way. Now when I spy Lena's trunk under Wynemah's bed I am reminded not of grief but of recovery. Lena's life after breast cancer and divorce proved that you can pick yourself up after creeping home in fear and self-doubt. She was, once again, my role model.

Harry Wood was unable to manage the family business on his own. First—in 1919—he lost Wellesley. He moved into his maternal grandfather's seventeenth-century stone house nearby in Natick. Harry's grandfather, Peter Hurd, had owned a fleet of clipper ships in the eighteenth century during the China trade. I traveled with him in my imagination. Sea Captain Peter Hurd filled his house and those of his children with furniture and china from around the world. I grew up with a smattering of those things. At this moment red-orange tulips with yellow tips droop over the edge of a tall cylindrical vase painted in Chinese red and soft blue designs that Peter brought back from one of his trips. Other days, one iris stands tall in an unglazed red clay tripartite vase carved in relief with snarling dragons.

But most of all I have traveled around the world with "Peter Hurd's sea captain's chest with the original rope handles"—as the chest was invariably referred to in the family. Lena used the chest to move between Wellesley in the summer and Boston in the fall for the opera season, then on to Florida for the winter months to protect her tubercular lungs from the Massachusetts cold. But it is not those travels that I imagined, but rather the exotic ones. The ones where Peter Hurd loaded his ship with treasure, then sailed back to Boston, stopping along the way to trade for leather in Spain or sugar in Cuba or tobacco in Virginia, yet always saving something for the family, like the plates I have with the persimmon-orange designs, or the vases or the floe blue.

Peter Hurd's sea chest is magnificent to behold in this day of fourth- and fifth- and sixth-growth trees. His chest—or trunk as we would more likely call it today—is made from thick slices of mahogany two and three feet wide. The top is flat—the better to stack. The sides are straight. The rope handles are thick. Hints of white cotton still encircle their girth. That chest opened the world for me. When I studied geography in grade school I pictured the chest being carried up the narrow steps from Peter Hurd's cabin and down the open plank onto the wharves of Amsterdam and Lisbon and even Gibraltar. When I later learned about clipper ships I went home and sat on the chest and imagined the flux and flow of the waves, the tilt in the trunk top as the ship slid into a shallow trough. When I read books about the China trade I opened the cupboards where Mother kept special dishes and pictured those treasures tucked among Peter Hurd's long white nightshirts in the chest. When I learned about the opium wars

Cassius "Cash" Clay as U.S. ambassador to Russia, c. 1860 (ABOVE); his cousin Henry "The Great Compromiser" Clay in Washington (BELOW).

Wedding picture of John Mavity Burns and
Keziah "Kizzie" Byce Clay, 1843.

Kizzie Clay's house in Prestonsburg, Kentucky, was used as Garfield's headquarters during the Battle of Middle Creek in January 1862.

Captain Frank Mott in cavalry division uniform, 1862.

(LEFT) *Catharine "Kate" Rebecca Burns, oldest child of John Burns and Kizzie Clay, near the time of her marriage to Frank Mott in 1869.*

(RIGHT) *Lena Leota Mott in her mid-twenties, c. 1900.*

Lee Mott with her husband, Charles Bishop (right), and friend in New York, c. 1900.

*Wynemah Ruby Mott when
she was eighteen, 1904.*

*Wendell William Meinhart
shortly after his marriage
to Wynemah, c. 1906.*

Wynemah and Wendell with Baby "Katie Carrie," 1908.

"Katie Carrie" and her mother, Wynemah, 1909.

∽

*Lena Mott and Harry Wood's estate, Wellesley,
in Wellesley, Massachusetts, c. 1909.*

(ABOVE) *Kate Burns Mott's "elegant gem of small-town splendor" in Ceredo, West Virginia, 1910.*

∾

(RIGHT) *Little "Katie Carrie" and her grandfather Frank Mott on the porch of the Ceredo home, 1910.*

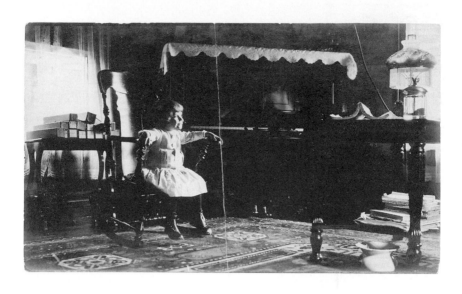

"Katie Carrie" in the sitting room of the "elegant gem," 1910.

∾

Wynemah, with arms folded, with her German in-laws. From left to right:
Caroline Meinhart, two neighbors, Wynemah, Kate Mott,
Kate Meinhart with "Katie Carrie," Ann Meinhart, Fay Meinhart, 1910.

Catharine
Meinhart Bateman's
grandfather
Wendell Ohlinger
Meinhart in Knights
Templar garb.

Christening picture
of the author with her
mother, Catharine, in
Clement Bateman's
gentleman's chair, 1940.

*Catharine and Bob
with Baby Katie in
Middletown, Ohio, 1941.*

*Katie and Dick
with Bob on
last Christmas
in Corbin,
Kentucky, 1948.*

Bob Bateman at age fifty.

Frank Maynard Bateman,
Bob's father, c. 1905.

Anna Highland Bateman,
Bob's mother, c. 1900.

Cousins Bob (right) and Dick
in matching outfits, c. 1914.

(LEFT) *Clement Cullen Bateman,*
Bob's grandfather, with his favorite
hunting spaniel on his front porch
in Washington Courthouse,
Ohio, c. 1909.

Cousins Bob (right)
and Dick with
their grandmother
Sarah Jane
"Jennie" Bell
Bateman,
c. 1916.

Catharine's Cape Cod cottage, her "dream house,"
in Ashland, Kentucky, 1939.

Catharine's Century House in Catlettsburg, Kentucky, 1959.

(ABOVE) *Katie, age thirteen, and Dick, age ten, with Catharine on Kizzie Clay's couch.*

∾

(LEFT) *Richard "Dick" Miller Bateman at age nineteen, 1963.*

*Catharine's home with Silas William Hearne from 1976 to 1998
in Ashland, Kentucky.*

*Catharine's Fiftieth Year Anniversary Ceremony as a member of the
Daughters of the American Revolution with her daughter, Katherine, 1985.*

Mount Sterling House, 1999.

I was embarrassed and chagrined and tried to forget where the chest had been.

With the exception of the Hurd and Wood pieces that Lena chose to save—like the sea chest and the vases and chinaware and the tiny, delicately carved ivory stork that sits on my bedroom chest and has since I can remember—Harry lost everything. According to the family, the loss was partially due to theft. In Harry's weakened financial state, his former sister-in-law, Lee Mott Bishop, got Harry to sell her his family's paintings, china, silver, and furniture at well below their true market value. Plus, for her so-called concern, he gave her—and she modestly accepted—many other prize pieces. The fine oil painting of a horse by an English artist that hung over the mahogany sideboard in the dining room went to Lee. China, crystal, silver, an inlaid Chippendale table all went to Lee that summer Lena spent recuperating from surgery and divorce in Ceredo. The family never forgave Lee. Kate supposedly said after Lee's most treacherous antic, "That's it. I wash my hands of her." And she did.

Uncle Harry Wood does live on in our family through a book he gave to his "Little Piffle," my mother. It is the 1881 one-volume edition of Lewis Carroll's *Alice's Adventures in Wonderland and Through the Looking Glass* with illustrations by John Tenniel. The volume is leather bound and gold tipped. The cover is a faded rose with images of Tenniel's Alice and the Cheshire Cat circled in black and embossed in gold. Inside on the flyleaf is the provenance of the book's ownership. "Mary E Wood" is scrawled a third of the page down. Under that in Harry's hand is an inscription to Mother: "To Piffle from Uncle Harry Sept 16/19." Below in Mother's familiar backhand is "Catharine Meinhart. Please read and return." If I were to treat the book the way the family treats some of its silver pieces—with the initials of each owner scaling down the face of a coffee urn or tea service—I would add my name, then my daughter's and her daughter's. But I will not do that. Instead, *Alice's Adventures* always sits proudly facing out on one of my bookshelves wherever I live, and I smile to think of Mother when she was still Uncle Harry's Piffle—before she was my mother.

After Lena got back on her feet following the surgery—and despite the divorce and the loss of Wellesley—she headed back to Boston to try to save the paint company from bankruptcy. She was unable to stop the downward financial spiral, though, and the family company was sold in 1921. Harry died penniless. Lena supported him as much as she could; Lee gave him nothing. Yet, while Lena was trying so desperately to hold the business together and—as the story goes—sitting in the same spot where Harry Wood first saw her, Lena became the star of another story. She met Uncle Irving.

Joseph Irving Hornbeck was a super salesman who covered the Wood's Paint Company. According to the story, Irving Hornbeck took one look at Lena sitting at that desk and said, "By God, Helena, I'm going to take you out of this mess and marry you some day." And he did. But eventually he put her into another mess just as bad.

I always pictured Irving as a suave Burt Lancaster. Based on his skills in marketing and sales, as well as his charming personality, he was hired by Havoline Oil Company in Washington, D.C. He and Lena moved to Connecticut Avenue and he quickly moved to the top of the firm. Soon Irving was hired away from Havoline by Atlantic Richfield Oil Company, and he and Lena returned to Boston. Mother's summers now were spent swimming from the boat dock of their summer home on Massachusetts Bay and eating fresh lobster and exotic foods cooked by their West Indies maid.

Irving was successful in more than sales and marketing. He also speculated in the stock market and fared well for a number of years. He was, however, also a gambler and a drinker. Mother periodically would tell the story about the summer night Irving came home late. He was drunk and without his car, but he had money of all denominations sticking out of every pocket. As did many wealthy businessmen in the 1920s, Irving overextended himself in the stock market. He lost his money in the 1929 crash. Irving lost Lena's money as well, except for a small bank account—an account he was not aware of—that she maintained in her own name. Soon after the stock market crash, Irving was fired from Ashland Richfield Oil because of his fiery temper. With Lena's tiny nest egg they purchased a house in Coral Gables, Florida, where Lena lived—and Wynemah and Mother visited—the rest of her life.

Despite Lena's delight when she was with Wynemah and Mother, there was a poignant quality about her—a hint of sadness that I sometimes saw in her eyes. When I was young I thought it probably had to do with losing Uncle Harry twice or with the whispered words about breast cancer. As I started to date I wondered if it was because she had lost the first man she loved—the one who gave her syphilis and the cupid-bow scar. Or maybe it was because Uncle Irving lost her money and their house. When I started to have children I decided the look I saw in Lena—the hint of melancholy that hovered just behind her eyes—was because she'd lost her baby and was never able to have another.

I will never know what Aunt Lena carried as her greatest sadness. What I do know is that as much as I idolized Lena, I was also unsettled by her presence. I was ten when Mother disclosed a scandalous secret to me. It was this: Mother loved her "Auntie" more than she loved her mother. I was impressionable. I was introspective. I was too young to be told such a thing, too young to be forced to hide forever Mother's second-best love for my beloved grandmother.

Each time a new letter arrived from Lena, Wynemah would read the letter aloud to Mother and me as soon as we gathered in the late afternoon. While I sat in that intimate circle of grandmother, mother, daughter, and aunt, sat in the fall of light from my grandmother's reading lamp listening to Lena's thrilling tales of daily life, I knew. I knew that Mother and Wynemah were living a lie—a lie that disturbed and frightened me. I also knew that I had my own secret. I, too, was living a lie, for I loved my grandmother more than I loved my mother. I was filled with guilt—even though it was Mother's own admission that allowed me to even begin to face the truth.

Lena Leota Mott Wood Hornbeck died in 1951 at age seventy-five in Coral Gables. Wynemah was sixty-five, Mother was forty-four, and I was eleven. In many ways Lena represented the confluence of the Clay and Cecil lines. She was tall and lean like her Clay cousins Henry and Cassius. She had the Clay nose and disparagingly compared her likeness to pictures of Henry Clay. She once painted a portrait of Henry in oil that she thought looked like her, a portrait that I now have tucked away in a closet. At the same time she had the poise and self-possession that would have made her great-grandmother Rebecca Cecil proud. I grew up—despite my grandmother's temper tantrums—with Rebecca Cecil's adage that no matter what happened in life "one should handle oneself with class." Lena personified that to me.

I have two happy reminders of my relationship with my great-aunt. As with many of the gifts linking the generations of our family one to the other, my childhood link to Lena is a book she gave me before I was five and reading. The book, published in 1917, is *The Funny Little Book* by Johnny Gruelle. I can remember sitting against Lena's bony body while she read it to me the first time and against my father's chest for successive readings until I could "read it" myself from memory. Later I held my own children against me while I read it to one, then two, and finally three of them and again to each of my grandchildren.

The book is now somewhat ragged. The once-white paper has turned to warm ivory. The edges of the pages are stained a sugar-syrup brown from the residual oil of each generation of tiny fingers. There are creases where each of us tried to turn the page, to rush the reader to the next set of bold, bright pictures. Some of the pages broke loose from the narrow spine when my children were small, and the thread that binds the rest to the boards looks weary. But one part of the book is fully intact. This nearly hidden page—the inside cover—was the most magic part of this little storybook. On it is a pencil sketch of Raggedy Ann drawn by Gruelle in 1933. Raggedy Ann stands with hair all askew on a flowered path that leads in twists and turns up a slope to a cottage set among flowering shrubs and trees. A bird has just landed on Raggedy Ann's outstretched hand, and she is smiling her painted smile as her black-button eyes glance sideways toward the bird.

Another memory of Lena keeps her close to me—a gold bracelet that I have worn for over forty years. "Lena L. Wood" is inscribed in a flowery script on this rose gold bangle that slides up and down my wrist each day. Tiny indentations march helter-skelter across the bracelet's smooth surface. These tiny dimples record the latest history of our family, for this bracelet is our family's version of a teething ring. Starting with Mother, four generations have held this bracelet in our tiny hands and let the cool metal soothe our swollen gums. Since Lena gave her treasure to her sister Wynemah when Mother was teething, each Cecil mother has worn the bracelet during her childbearing years. Although my daughter wore it when her children were small, she lets me wear it now, for she knows that this bracelet is my talisman. It keeps Lena, my role model, close. Still, it will move on to my granddaughter when the time comes.

I kept Mother's secret about her love for her "Auntie" for the rest of my grandmother's life. I feel certain Wynemah never knew that she was second best. If she did, I am not sure that she would have cared. She was possessive and controlling toward Mother, but I do not know if she ever really loved her. Frank Mott had a saying about his children with Kate that was repeated to me time and again. "I may have raised four devils, but at least I raised no fools." My grandmother, Wynemah Ruby, the third beauty, was indeed no fool. But neither was she a devil in the whimsical sense her father meant. Her fiery temperament was too mean-spirited to be referred to with caprice. Each of the generations that she touched had to learn to deal with her.

11

THE LITTLE INDIAN

WYNEMAH RUBY Mott Meinhart was undeniably a beauty. But looks were not everything. She was high strung from the beginning, strong-willed but thin-skinned and easily hurt. She did not take criticism well, and, even as an adult, a negative response to something she said would elicit an indignant response: "Are you disputing my word?" Her sharp tongue wounded most of her friends at one time or another. But Wynemah's quick wit and charismatic charm invariably pulled her lost friends back into her fold.

Wynemah's sister Lena raised her; Kate was done with child rearing. Wynemah's half-siblings from Kate and Frank's previous marriages were grown and married by the time Wynemah was born, and her older sister Lee would have nothing to do with her. So it was up to Lena, ten years old at the time of the birth, to love and nurture her baby sister. Lena and Wynemah formed a bond during those years that was never broken.

Wynemah rarely mentioned her mother. There was the rescue story about Kate grabbing Wynemah's feet when Ida Lee dragged her down the stairs by the hair. And there were wry references to Kate's favoritism, to the fact that the Crown Prince could do no wrong. Most of the time, though, when Wynemah talked about her mother it was about the year Kate spent upstairs. That fall, when Wynemah was not quite twelve—that fall when Kate walked up those imposing front stairs and did not come down—changed my grandmother's life forever.

The story came out in bits and pieces as I was growing up. Sometimes, when she was teaching me to keep house, Wynemah would remember how she had to fill the lamps with kerosene and clean the lamp chimneys every day in Kate's bedroom so her mother could read. Other times she would tell how she had to empty her mother's chamber pot before she went off to school and then as soon as she got home. She would talk about library books—dropping off some and picking up others, books on Kate's long list of favorites and things still to read—and how she had to keep Kate supplied with daily newspapers, bourbon, and homemade wine.

Sometimes, but not often, Wynemah would speak of the other thing that happened that year when she was twelve, something worse than Kate's withdrawal from the family. Sadly, in those rare moments of deep reflection, she would talk about the time when Lena—her real mother—left home to join Lee in New York. Lena did not want to leave her, Wynemah always said, especially at this time when both Lena and Wynemah were trying to hold the house together. Yet Lee persisted. Finally Lena, age twenty-two, opted to wrench herself out of Kate's stifling grip in order to start a life of her own—even if it meant leaving her baby sister.

Wynemah confessed she cried every night for months after Lena left. By herself, now, she took care of Kate, did the family laundry, and helped her aging father prepare meals. But most of all she tried to make up for Kate's absence to Frank and her older, pampered brother, Glen.

Wynemah was nearly thirteen when her mother walked without warning back down the wide front stairs under the brass chandelier hanging from the blue ceiling. There was no fanfare. Wynemah, like Mother, did not see Kate's year upstairs as abnormal behavior. Kate was selfish and spoiled, and this was simply a manifestation of those traits. Kate slipped back into the household as if nothing had happened. But something had happened. Wynemah had changed. Traits had incubated over that year that soon took full form.

Kate had never mothered Wynemah, yet Wynemah had been forced to mother Kate that year. And what Wynemah decided at that inappropriate age for mothering was that she did not like the role. In fact, she hated it. Further, during Kate's year upstairs Wynemah determined that no one appreciated what she was doing, that no one cared how hard it was for her to go to school and take care of the family, or how difficult it was to maintain order in the house. Wynemah never outgrew those perceptions. For the rest of her life she felt that most of what she did for others was unacknowledged, unappreciated. The combination of these two traits—a dislike for mothering and a tendency toward martyrdom—did not bode well for her daughter and only child—my mother, Catharine Carolyn Meinhart.

Wynemah met my German grandfather, Wendell William Meinhart, in 1905 when they were both eighteen. Wendell lived and worked in Ashland, and Wynemah lived ten miles away in

Ceredo, West Virginia, but streetcars crossed the bridge over the Big Sandy River at Cliffside, where teenagers gathered in groups to dance in the summer and ice skate in the winter.

Wynemah and Wendell met in Cliffside. It was winter, and the ice rink reverberated with the deep thumps of a small band and the treble scores of a hundred skate blades. I can picture my grandfather clearly on the day my grandparents first saw each other. Wendell had blue eyes, and his shapely head was capped in blond curls. He was of medium height and slender in build. But most of all I can see how lithe he was, for, as the story goes, he took one look at beautiful Wynemah, wrapped in her long coat with the collar of soft fur that fluffed like cygnet down around her shapely chin, and began to skate figure eights around her. I can see her eyes flash with the smile she was trying to hide—the way those eyes always did when she knew someone was admiring her—and I watch him doing those figure eights around and around her, stopping only when she agreed to skate with him.

When I was young I loved to look at Wendell's scuffed-up skates, which hung by their tattered laces at the top of my grandparents' steep basement stairs. Each time I saw them I would ask Wynemah to tell me the story about the figure eights. As I got older and began to be courted myself, the story took on a warm, romantic glow. Even though by then Wendell had only a fringe of silky, snow-white curls and had grown quite round, I still saw him the way he looked that first day he spied dark-eyed Wynemah and sped toward her across the ice.

There was, however, a darker side to my grandparents' courtship that I discovered when I was older. Mother hinted at it. Wynemah stayed mute on the subject. But Wendell fully disclosed it in letters he wrote to his intended the year of their engagement—love letters found tucked away in Wynemah's lingerie drawer after she died. In those letters, which I kept in my bedside table drawer for years beside love letters of my own, I discovered Wendell's heartache over Wynemah's ongoing flirtations with other young men who flocked to her house in Ceredo. Although the early letters are full of love and excitement over their engagement, Wendell begins to question some of Wynemah's actions in June 1905, four months before they are to be married.

Ashland Ky June 2, 1905

Miss Wynemah Mott
Ceredo WstVa

My dear girl,

Received your short missive this P.M. and of course was delighted with one exception and that is the fact that I cannot see you Sunday afternoon but if you must have it that way guess it will have to be. You said if it rained I could come up. Now—I like that, makes me think you are using me for a second hand man but perhaps I will see you at Cliffside if it dont rain. Hope you will not be with any fellows . . .

Later in June Wendell voices his concerns over Wynemah's continuing dealings with a former beau, Harry Olilinger.

Ashland, Ky June 27, 1905

Miss Wynemah Mott
Ceredo, WstVa

My dear Wynemah

Received your short but sweet letter this evening and think you might have written more as you should have had all evening before you.

You said you have been thinking of me all day. Well Kid if what had passed through your brain as did mine I suppose you would have gone crazy and Wynemah I have come to one point that you let Hurry Olilinger drop altogether or let me. For he has carried things too darn far to suit me. . . .

I am going to bring your affair with him to an end or bring this affair of mine to an end for my life has been nothing but misery for the last three weeks and I cant stand it any longer. . . . Wynemah don't think because we are engaged that we cant separate for if I should hear anything two days before we are married I will quit, for you know how bitterly opposed I am to deceitfulness. . . .

Yours

Wendell

A crisis looms again a month later.

Ashland, Ky July 25, 1905

Miss Wynemah Mott
Ceredo, WstVa

My dearest Wynemah,

Once more I sit here writing to the girl who I once loved but I have begun to think she has ceased to love me and has gone to another but hope you can be truer to him then you have been to me, if he asks for steady company.

Wynemah what ever made you do such a trick after I warned you and after what you said to me the last time it occurred?

Wendell and Wynemah pass the second deception crisis, but Wendell continues to doubt through the late summer and fall:

Well dearie this is dance night and we are not there. At least I am not, and hope you are not. Or, . . . you have played me false once but hope it will never happen again for it almost broke my heart the last time although you wont believe it.

There is a story about my grandparents relating to this period. According to Mother, Wendell took a streetcar from Ashland to Ceredo to see Wynemah two nights before the wedding. She was not expecting him. Sometimes Mother said it was an innocent trip; other times she said that Wendell still did not trust his bride-to-be. As he came in view of her house he saw her sitting on the porch steps arm in arm with her former beau, Harry Olilinger. He turned around and went back without being seen. Nor, according to the story, did he disclose to Wynemah that he had been there.

Despite this hurt—if the story is true—Wendell William Meinhart married Wynemah Ruby Mott on October 30, 1905. Wynemah had turned nineteen three days before, Wendell a month earlier. As I gently refolded each love letter that Wynemah had hidden away for sixty years I could hear the pleasing tenor voice of my honest, gentle grandfather. But I also could hear my grandmother's standard response to any question she did not want to answer: "Ask me no secrets and I'll tell thee no lies."

Wynemah scandalized her German in-laws, she told me with pride. Wendell came from a second-generation German family whose Meinhardt, Ebersbach, and Sauer relatives had come to America to escape the German draft in the late 1840s and early 1850s. They settled in German communities on both sides of the Ohio River near Cincinnati, Ohio. Around 1880 Wendell's father, Wendell Ohlinger Meinhardt, followed his older brother, Valentine, up the Ohio River to Ashland.

The Meinharts (by the time I was born the "d" had been dropped from the Meinhardt name) had done well both in Ohio and in Kentucky. Pharmacy was the career of choice for the sons, with their training financed by astute investments in real estate. The family owned property throughout Ashland's business district—including the major drugstores in town. They also had developed much of the residential property in the wide Ohio River valley where Ashland's early residents made their homes. Throughout my childhood as we drove past the gracious lawns and turreted houses near downtown Ashland, Mother would point and say, "Grandmother and Grandfather Meinhart built that house"—or that house or that house. Wendell's family was financially comfortable, predictably stable, and—according to their new daughter-in-law—inordinately boring. Wynemah did not fit in.

First, she rollerskated when she was eight months pregnant. She skated down the wide limestone sidewalks past block after cultured block of rambling Victorian houses built by the Meinharts, past houses filled with Meinhart sisters and brothers, aunts and uncles, and the Presbyterian and Episcopalian leaders of the community. Her mother-in-law scolded her in German and earned Wynemah's scorn, but she did not stop skating.

Further, she did not like her sisters-in-law, Ann, Kate, and Fay. They had no character, she said, and they had nothing in common to discuss; in fact, according to Wynemah, Wendell's sisters hardly talked at all. All they did was cook and clean. When they did talk, Wynemah invariably got her feelings hurt. I can remember months—sometimes years—when Wynemah would not speak to one or another of them, would ignore them completely at birthdays and Christmas, would refer to them as "dumb Krauts." She did, however, like Wendell's brothers and especially his somewhat eccentric and very rich uncle, Col.—as in the honorific Kentucky Colonel—Valentine C. Meinhart Junior.

Finally, Wynemah scandalized her German in-laws because she did not want to raise a brood of children, did not want to be a mother at all. Little Catharine Carolyn, my mother, was born on November 6, 1907, when Wynemah was barely twenty-one. She had not been planned. "Giving birth is the worst thing that can ever happen to you," Wynemah said in Catharine's birth story, a story that she repeated to both Mother and me from our childhoods on. Wynemah's labor was so long and so painful that she broke two—two—leather straps tied to the bedposts to help with the pain. Those hours in the birthing bed were so abhorrent, so repugnant, so undignified that she swore she would never have another child. Nor should we—Mother and I—"even consider" having children.

Although Mother and I ignored Wynemah's admonition, my grandmother kept the promise she made to herself on that early November day in 1907. I do not know why Mother chose to tell me about Wynemah's second pregnancy, nor do I remember the circumstances that prompted the telling. I do remember that I was in my late teens and that we were in my grandmother's living room and that Wynemah was upstairs changing clothes. I also know that Mother was nervous and that she made me promise before she even began to disclose "the secret" that I would never let my grandmother know I knew what she was about to say. Mother was not even sure that Wynemah knew that Catharine knew what Wynemah had done.

After this prolonged and uncomfortable prologue, which had taken me from mild curiosity to growing nervousness to palpable, heart-thumping anxiety—and after Mother walked to the stairs, listened for a moment, and then closed the door at their foot—she told me the following story. A few years after Mother was born, Wynemah got pregnant a second time. She did not want the child, the pain, the inconvenience. She wanted to have an abortion. But Wendell refused. He wanted another child. He wanted a son as well as his daughter. He wanted a son to hunt and fish with. So Wynemah took the matter into her own hands. She threw herself down a steep flight of stairs.

Wynemah survived but the baby did not. According to Mother, who at this stage in the story was whispering, Wynemah was far enough along in the pregnancy to determine that she had aborted a baby boy. She said that Wendell never fully forgave his beautiful young wife. Wynemah had a hysterectomy in her early thirties. There would be no more unwanted pregnancies. She made sure of that.

I was haunted by this story as a teenager. There were steep stairs in the house my grandparents lived in. Were these the stairs? Or were there other stairs where Wynemah felt she could kill the baby but not herself? I often stood at the top of the stairs in her house and wondered what it would be like to be so desperate that you would do what she did. At those moments, when the late afternoon light from the window behind me silhouetted my shape and made it stretch down, down toward the bottom of those long stairs, I would try to imagine what my grandmother was thinking the moment before she leaned far out into the fall. Was she afraid of broken bones, did she think she might disfigure her beautiful face, did she weigh the possibility that she might die? I wondered if she ever felt regret, ever felt guilty, ever felt sorry for what she took away from my grandfather.

I never knew the answers to these questions because I kept my promise to Mother; Wynemah never learned that I knew that horrible story. But when I think about it now I wonder if she despaired so deeply over the unwanted pregnancy that she did not care if she died along with the baby. And it's only recently occurred to me that my grandmother's desperate attempt to abort might be connected to something my mother told me, also in secret, a few years after she told me the stairs story.

During one of her summer visits with Lena at Wellesley, Wynemah met and fell deeply in love with a man from Boston. They were each in their mid-twenties. She was married. He was single. The love affair continued for several years through letters during the winter months and time together in the summer. He waited summer after summer for Wynemah to leave Wendell. Wynemah told him she would ask for a divorce, but she never did, which "broke his heart." Several years after Wynemah ended their relationship, her lover married someone else. His first child was a daughter. He named her Wynemah.

Mother told me this story in a distanced, bare-bones manner, and I processed it in an equally distanced way. What I now wonder is this: Did Wynemah suspect the baby she carried was her lover's and not her husband's? And if she did, was she afraid her affair would be exposed? The family had stepped in to protect the other two beauties when their sexual escapades could no longer be hidden. Who was going to protect her? Perhaps when she stood at the top of those stairs and leaned out until she fell, she was so desperate to hide a secret that she did not care what happened to her. And maybe, when she told me over and over, "You are from a long line of strong women and you will be strong like all the rest . . . ," she was thinking not just of Sisters Lena and Lee but also of herself. She knew that when the family did not circle around her, she was able to take matters into her own hands.

What made Mother tell me stories about my grandmother that put her in such a bad light? She was definitely conflicted about telling some of them. "Mother must never know I told you this," she would say. Even when I was a child I knew I was in the middle of a tug-of-war between my grandmother and my mother. Each wanted my sympathy and my undivided love. I loved Wynemah. I wanted to live with her and my grandfather. When I was ten I asked Wynemah to adopt me. When Mother found out—for Wynemah could not let the triumph of this request go unacknowledged—Mother unsealed her storybook regarding her life with her mother.

Catharine knew her birth story—the two broken leather straps, the "worst pain," the "never again." And sometimes she would talk about her early years with me. Quietly, as if it had happened to someone else, she would recite a litany of her mother's stock phrases during sudden outbursts of temper: "I hate you!" "I wish you had never been born!" "You have ruined my life!" One time, according to Mother, Wendell's Uncle Valentine was present during one of Wynemah's angry tirades. He said—in front of young Catharine—"Wynemah, that child is going to have problems for the rest of her life if you keep saying those things to her." Wynemah did not listen to the only Meinhart relative she truly liked, and Catharine never lost her fear of her mother or her underlying guilt for being born. The only thing that saved her, she said, was the knowledge that she was loved—truly loved—by her father and her dear "Auntie" Lena.

Photographs tell the story. Catharine's childhood was well documented. There are snapshots of her nestled in her grandfather Frank Mott's lap, pictures of "the baby" rocked by her grandmother Kate, pictures of her on Wendell's shoulders, and pictures taken at Wellesley over successive summers with Lena. In all of these pictures the lens captures happy moments. Not so with the pictures of little "Katie Carrie" with her mother. In each of those snapshots Mother is pulling away. None—at least none that were kept in photo albums—show her leaning into her mother in safe security as she did with her other relatives; none show her smiling up into her mother's face. Instead, Catharine is trying to draw away from Wynemah. The camera catches the tension between the mother and the daughter as Wynemah tries to forcibly hold Catharine in the frame.

Few bonds between mothers and daughters are free from conflict. Still, when I began my long trek back through my family's history, I was hopeful that the process of clean, objective research—a process that usually clears my head and drops historical clues into their proper slots—would erase the charged emotions I have held about the Clay and Cecil mothers since childhood. I wonder now—although I did not think this way when I began—if what I was really after was a scholarly clarification of the interactions between my grandmother and my mother. Although the historical blueprint of family behavior I have discovered so far illuminates certain patterns, it does not fully elucidate the relationship between Wynemah and Catharine, a relationship in which I was often central.

I feel certain that if correspondence or some other personal documentation existed that shed light on the relationships between the mothers and daughters in our early family, I would be better equipped to edit the stories about Wynemah and Catharine. Sadly, I do not have the luxury of those kinds of private accounts. There are no surviving letters written by Clay mothers in the seventeenth century that tell of family dramas like the one written by Elizabeth Bacon to her sister back in England describing her anguish over her husband Nathaniel Bacon's well-being. There are no remaining personal accounts in the eighteenth century chronicling Phoebe Belcher Clay's feelings when—at age seventeen—she left her mother to settle in the distant unsettled territories of Virginia's southwestern mountains. Nor is there a firsthand account of Phoebe's anguish when her daughter Tabitha and Tabitha's two brothers were massacred in 1783—only a description of that horrible event told by Phoebe's grandsons to a collector of early settlers' stories a century later.

I do know from family stories told about our nineteenth-century mothers and daughters that Kizzie Clay rushed home to her mother, Rebecca Cecil, when Garfield's staff tromped into her house in January 1862. I also know that Kizzie preferred to live with her mother rather than with her husband—preferred it, that is, until John Burns built Kizzie the fine house in Prestonsburg and later bought her another fine house in Catlettsburg. I do have Kate Burns's keepsake album in which her mother, Kizzie Clay, wrote nothing. Plus I know from family accounts—reinforced by Kate's move to Frankfort with her father in 1857—that Kate and her mother were not close. On the other hand, Kate made a decision to be buried next to her mother rather than next to her husband or her beloved father, and in so doing she erased an easy analysis of their relationship.

Catharine would make the same decision as her grandmother. Despite the fear she had of Wynemah throughout their lives together, she could never bear to pull away. Rather than purchase a plot beside her two sons, she chose to be entombed on the outside of a new mausoleum in Ashland's cemetery so, in her words, she could "look toward Mother and the mountains beyond." But much more transpired in Catharine's life before she reached that point.

12

CATHARINE AND ROBERT

CATHARINE CAROLYN Meinhart somehow survived her childhood with Wynemah and turned into a fun-loving teenager. There are albums of pictures of "The Nutty Five"—"Cat," as she was called then, standing shoulder to shoulder with her four best girlfriends. In those pictures her head is usually thrown back in laughter or her eyes are sparkling as she looks toward her high school sweetheart, Earl. Most of the pictures are from the summer of 1925, the summer following Catharine's graduation from high school, the last summer of her carefree youth—for things were about to change for both Catharine and Wynemah.

In the fall of 1925 Catharine left home for Mary Washington College in Fredericksburg, Virginia, but she did not stay there long. During the second term she left the college in a jealous fury, a caustic rage reminiscent of her mother's destructive outbursts. Catharine had discovered that in her absence her sweetheart Earl had been intimately involved with someone else. In spite, when she returned to Ashland, she too began to see someone else, and in her anger she upped the ante. She married her new beau. She was barely twenty. I knew nothing of this first marriage until I was in my early teens, and then Mother said little beyond that it had occurred. It was not until November 1980, the month Catharine turned seventy-three, that she decided to elaborate on the story of her marriage to Frederick Frank. She did it in writing so her grandchildren would have a record of her life—her part in the greater family account.

Ashland, Kentucky November 1980

About the first marriage there is little to tell for it was of little length. Three people were involved, painfully, Earl, the young love whom I spited by this marriage, the perfectly nice young fellow, Frederick Frank, who fell in love with me, but most painfully involved was myself for my unkindness to each of us.

Frederick, a Canadian, the son of Frederick Frank Sr., a dentist, was a friend of Dr. George Bell, an Ashland dentist who spent vacation times fishing in the northern lakes near Sudbury. With a chance for a ride to the sunny South, and the possibility of a job with Armco Steel that booming summer of '27, Frederick came to Ashland with Dr. Bell. . . . Our courtship was brief. January 28, 1928 we eloped to Ironton, Ohio where we were married in the Episcopal Church.

When my family heard the news in March my mother threw one of her wild tantrums and everybody in the family took cover including my new husband. I wanted very much to get away from home. I bought a drop leaf six-leg cherry table and a cherry corner cupboard. We rented an apartment on Ashland Avenue and were ready to move when Wynemah, with butter-melting warmth emerged from her

corner and urged us to buy two lots back of the home place on 3624
Spring Valley Drive in Old Orchard [a neighborhood just within
the southernmost boundary of Ashland] *and live at home until*
we had money to build a house. At this point the idea sounded not
only good but economical. I bought the lots for $100 each but life with
Mother had been the situation I was trying to escape. Thus was the
beginning of the ending of a marriage built on a weak foundation.

In the early spring of 1929 I went to Boston to visit my favorite
Auntie, Lena Hornbeck, to escape the daily actuality of a foolish and
loveless marriage. Thank God this marriage did not produce any
pregnancies. . . . I returned home, an unhappy wife to an unhappy
husband. He had had a night on the town and had contracted
gonorrhea. A trip to our doctor confirmed the diagnosis. I felt sorry
for Frederick but not sorry enough. He took a trip to Canada from
which he never returned. Divorce papers were filed the spring of '29
and I was once again free at the age of twenty-one.

Catharine did not give Frederick Frank a chance to return to
Ashland. As soon as he left for Canada she filed for divorce—
without his knowledge—on the grounds of infidelity. He learned
of his changed marital status when he received a copy of the final
divorce documents. I asked her about the speed of the divorce
and the fact that Frederick had no say in it. Catharine was defi-
ant. Her eyes flashed black and she said, "I did not want to be
married to him anymore!" Besides, she had already met my father,
Bob Bateman.

Catharine remembered in filmic detail the September day in
1928 when she first saw Bob Bateman.

As was the custom, a car full of girls with whom I spent my lei-
sure time was parked on Winchester Avenue in front of the First

National Bank building. Next door was Klein's Soda Fountain
where there was "the gathering of the clan." Bob and Al Slagel at
whose home Bob had taken a room walked out of Klein's, came
over to the car and Bob was given a round of introductions. He was
wearing gray Scottish tweed knickers, plaid wool knee socks upheld
with the red wool Scottish garters, a black slipover sweater with just
the edge of a white collar showing at the neck. His very thick black
hair was smoothed down in a side part. He had a straight perfect
nose and rather a full sensual mouth. Curiously startling were his
sparkling black eyes, almost almond shaped. Without being hand-
some there was a certain "damn-Yankee" gentility which made him
a standout in our southern-almost-Appalachian culture. Within
my hearing someone remarked, "It is too bad Catharine is married
for Robert Bateman would be a good catch for her." And as I saw
Robert Bateman walking toward me that September day I thought,
"Yes, it is too bad" for there was an instant feeling of rapport which
we later discussed.

After Catharine divorced Frederick, she and Bob began to
see one another. They were married a year later on April 5, 1930.
"I can't remember whose family was the most unhappy over our
marriage, Bob's or mine," she wrote in 1980. "I did win over his
family but he never won over Mother."

Wynemah had considerably more to say to me throughout my
childhood on the subject of Catharine's marriage to Bob Bateman—whom she relentlessly referred to as "that goddamned
bastard your father." According to her, she "knew from the beginning that Bob Bateman was a ne'er-do-well." He may have been
well bred, she admitted, and he may have come from money, but
he was a "damned Yankee from Ohio who did not know how to
stick with anything, even a job at American Rolling Mill that was

handed to him on a silver platter because of his family connections." He expected everything to fall neatly in his lap. And, to prove his lack of discipline—and this is the only story I was ever told about my parent's wedding—"Bob got drunk at the reception and threw up in the front yard. At his own wedding," my grandmother always said, "in front of everyone!"

Further, Wynemah blamed Bob for the breakup of Catharine's first marriage. While Catharine was in Boston with Lena, Wynemah's story went, it was Bob who talked Frederick into going out on the town. It was Bob who got him drunk and fixed him up with a whore. It was Bob who gave Catharine an excuse for divorce so he could marry her himself. "But Catharine would not listen to me," Wynemah said. "Oh, no. Your mother was so gullible. She thought Bob Bateman hung the moon. No matter what he did she still loved him—she still loves him to this day. Still loves him, despite everything that happened later."

Robert Eugene Bateman, like Catharine, was an only child. This fact—uncommon at the time—defined them within their peer group of large sprawling families. It later also defined my brother Dick and me, for we often had to explain to our friends why, unthinkably in clan-like Kentucky, we had no cousins. Bob and Catharine, however, had more in common than their lack of siblings. They shared a worldview and pride regarding their family histories.

Bob's family was overflowing with genealogists. Packets of documents and genealogy data were saved to prove the long pedigree charts made for each of us: "Katie's Charts," "Dick's Charts," etc. I have boxes of pictures in tiny pressed leather frames all neatly labeled and packed together. There are military records from several generations, including an exchange of letters in 1855 between my great-great-great-great-grandmother and the Department of the Interior regarding a land warrant owed to her husband for his participation in the War of 1812. I have jewelry that belonged to my Bateman relatives, and sterling silver, and furniture. Books of genealogy have been published—and updated regularly—to record the family's marriages, christenings, their movements toward Ohio, their involvement in each of America's wars. I have pictures of generations of gravestones in Ohio and Virginia and Pennsylvania.

Interestingly, the family line that took center stage for the Batemans was not Bob's relatives from Great Britain, but those from Switzerland, the Backenstosses, who arrived in Philadelphia aboard the *St. Andrew* on October 7, 1743. The leader of the group was Hans Ulrich Backenstoss—a mason by trade who was nearly fifty when he emigrated. With him were his wife, six of their children, a nephew, Hans's sister-in-law, who was the wife of his deceased brother, and her two sons. All had been born in Rafz, Switzerland, as had their parents and grandparents before them. This small kinship group migrated first to Bern, Pennsylvania, then to Augusta County, Virginia, and on to Washington Courthouse, Ohio—where the Backenstosses—now Backenstoes—finally settled.

My father did not like to talk about his family. "It made him sad," Mother always said. But I knew some basic information about his immediate family. I knew that his father, my grandfather Frank Maynard Bateman, was an attorney who had worked with President Harding when Harding was still an Ohio senator and lieutenant governor. I also knew that Frank had been an executive at the American Rolling Mill Company—Armco Steel—in Middletown, Ohio, and that he had a strong tenor voice. He died of a kidney disorder in 1919 when Bob was ten. Four years later Bob's mother, Anna May Highland Bateman, died. His aunt—

Frank's only sister, Ada Bell Bateman Miller—and her husband, Horace Miller, raised him after his mother's death. He was angry, Mother said, because they'd sent him away to Sewanee Military Academy in Tennessee after his mother died and because he had not been trusted to control his sizeable trust fund until he was twenty-five.

Only now, through my research, have I gained a wider picture of my father's ancestry and childhood. In a drawer full of old documents and flaking, treacle-colored newspaper clippings that had passed down to me, I found the military records of each Backenstoss, Backenstoe, Bell, and Bateman who fought in each one of our country's wars—one family member for every war since the Revolution. But more important to understanding Bob was the material about his mother's family—the Highlands. I had genealogy papers that trace the Highland family back to Pennsylvania in the eighteenth century—coldly impersonal pedigree charts that provided only a mechanical structure of the family. Yet I also had a packet of folded and crackled newspaper clippings that had been tucked away among the more official Bateman documents. They turned out to be obituaries from the *Washington Register*, Washington Court House, Ohio, and it was through these dreary descriptions of one death after another in Bob's mother's family that I finally got to know my father.

As I read these death notices, I came to understand that my grandmother Anna May Highland Bateman came from a family with frighteningly fragile health, and that young Robert Eugene Bateman had already witnessed or been aware of several lingering family illnesses that eventually ended in death before he finally lost his own parents. The first obit I read was that of Bob's mother, my grandmother, published in April 1923. It told how she had been sick for two years before she died, that she and her husband, Frank

Maynard Bateman, had lived in Middletown for eight years, that after Frank died in 1919 Anna had moved back to Washington Court House to be near her mother and her Highland relatives. For four years she and her young son Bob lived in Washington Court House. One month before she died, her doctors moved her to the Middletown City Hospital. And then the lines, "It is to her son, Robert Bateman, age fourteen years, that the most sincere sympathy is extended. He attended the local high school [in Washington Court House] until his mother was taken to the hospital. Since that time he has made his home with his uncle and aunt, Mr. and Mrs. Horace O. Miller, in Middletown."

For the first time I felt the grief and bewilderment my father must have experienced with the death of one parent and then the other. From his earliest memories he had lived in Middletown in a happy, prosperous home. His aunt and uncle and his first cousin, Richard Bateman Miller, who was more like a brother than a cousin, lived nearly next door. Then when he was ten his father died, and everything changed. Bob left Middletown for Washington Court House—where there were no cousins—and started a school life afresh. Two years later his mother became ill, frightening after the loss of his father. Over the next two years she slowly failed. When she was too sick to be cared for by the maid who lived with them, Bob was uprooted once again. He and his mother returned to Middletown—she to the hospital, Bob to live with his Aunt Ada, Uncle Hi, and cousin Dick. There in Middletown he watched his mother die.

The next obituary was that of Anna's only brother, Frank Tasso Highland, who died on July 1, 1903, when he was barely thirty-five. In this newspaper account I learned that "his father died when Frank was quite young, leaving his mother with five small children, of whom Frank was the oldest, and the only son. . . .

Frank and these three sisters were educated in the Ohio Soldiers' and Sailors' Orphans' Home at Xenia, Ohio. . . ."

My grandmother, then, like my father, had lost a father and had been raised—at least for a while—as an orphan. Unlike Bob, she had siblings, although, sadly, she outlived them all. One sister, Clara, died at age nine. Another, Ona Belle, died, after an illness of five years, just nine days before my father was born. The third, Mayme, died when Bob was nine. Mayme's obit reports that "for some months she had been in failing health, but was not despondent or discouraged; always making a brave fight for recovery for the sake of those she loved . . ."

Only Anna had lived to be fifty. Mayme was forty-five when she died, and Frank and Ona Belle were in their thirties. Little Clara had not made it to ten. None of the obituaries explain the cause of death, although tuberculosis was often mentioned in connection to the Highland side of my family—that and possibly cancer. Mother said Bob did not know what killed his mother, just that she was in pain.

I'd had no idea that my Highland relatives had such short lives. I did not even know that my grandmother Bateman had brothers and sisters. No one talked about that side of my family. Yet as I read the Highland obituaries over and over I began to piece together the layers of my father's early life. He'd had some happy times. I can track those times through the many pictures taken of Bob and his cousin Dick in their matching outfits—pictures of Independence Day celebrations, of boat trips with Armco Steel employees where each boy wore a white sailor suit, of both boys in tweed knickers when they were older, on horses, in Europe for their Grand Tour. Yet tucked in and around the fun of childhood there must have been grief. Anna was losing her family one by one.

It took several readings of the obituaries for me to realize that none of Anna's siblings had had children. My father was the only Highland grandchild. Finally I understood why he had not stayed in Washington Court House with his mother's family to finish high school as he had wanted, why he had resented being sent off to military school. Bob's grandmother Highland was seventy-five when he was orphaned. And there were no Highland aunts left to take care of him. The only relative able to take him in was his father's only sister, Ada, and her husband. Despite the presence of his cousin Dick, he never felt a valued part of their family.

I now believe that when Robert Eugene Bateman came to Ashland, Kentucky, in 1928 he carried emotional baggage filled with the knowledge of lingering family sicknesses that always ended in death. After his mother's death he had finished high school at Sewanee and spent a year at Miami College in Ohio. At nineteen he had come to Ashland to work at Armco Steel's plant on the Ohio River. He had come to start a life on his own terms.

I feel certain that when Bob met Catharine they felt an immediate spark between them. Perhaps over time, after Catharine divorced Frederick Frank and during their own courtship, Bob disclosed to her some of the sadness he carried with him. Maybe he was able to convey to Catharine what he felt when one, then another and again another of his family members died. It is unlikely that he said to Catharine that he had been scarred by it all, for people did not verbalize those things back then.

In her 1980 letter to her grandchildren Mother described her life with Bob. "Early on," she began, "I discovered I had married a self-centered man. My love was limitless, his was limited. Having known a loving father and remembering a happy growing-up I was almost subconsciously drawing comparisons."

She went on to describe turbulent years of alternating instability, fleeting happiness, drinking, and despair. "I can't say that there were not a lot of happy times, but there were a lot more unhappy times. Life with Bob was full of surprises, not all of them pleasant." At age twenty-five my father "got into and out of the Scottish terrier breeding business (at a sizeable loss) and into the business of being a father." Their first child, my brother Robert E. Bateman Junior, was born October 9, 1936, but "this greatly looked forward to child was with us a brief thirty-eight hours. . . . Bob took to his grief with the bottle and I took mine in tears." For consolation Bob and Cat built a Cape Cod cottage—Mother's "dream house." Yet Bob remained inconsolable. His drinking increased, and, Mother noted, "there were several trips to Lexington for a 'drying out' for my husband."

In the summer of 1939 Mother discovered, joyfully, that she was again pregnant, with me. Rather than sharing her joy, Bob asked her to get an abortion and to give him a divorce. Mother was so angry she threw a bowl of buttered peas at him, and refused both requests, suspecting by now that "there was a strong force of another woman behind him. . . . I was to find out that he was totally infatuated with a blond divorcee, the ex-wife of one of our neighbors."

Catharine first disclosed this requested abortion story to me when I was eleven. I was too young to hear it, and it was especially perplexing because Bob had been my major caregiver, the only parent I remember ever hugging me, kissing me, comforting me when I was scared or sad. It was he who toilet trained me, who taught me how to tie my shoes. He was the one I ran to for comfort.

Wynemah took Catharine's new dilemma with Bob into her own hands. True to form, she went to the upscale clothing store in

Charleston, West Virginia, where Bob's new love worked, pulled a leather whip out of her purse, cracked it in the air, and swore that if she ever heard of "that whore" seeing "that bastard" again she would "flay her in public."

When I picture this savage scene by a gleaming glass jewelry counter with polished chrome trim, I feel anxious for Garnett. (I learned her name a few years before Mother died when one of Mother's friends, in that furtive tone used only for off-color secrets, asked if Catharine knew "whatever happened to Garnett.") I fear that Garnett might stumble back and crash into the case of exquisite necklaces and bracelets. I worry because there is another strand to the twisted story. According to Wynemah, Garnett was also pregnant with Bob Bateman's child.

But the trip to the jewelry counter was not the only one Wynemah took that fateful day. Late in the afternoon she made a visit to Garnett's mother, who was the cook in a railroad-car diner on the edge of Ashland's business district. She told her that Catharine was pregnant and in her sweetest tones said there must be something that the two mothers could do. Garnett's mother said, according to the story, "That god-damned bastard. He said he was divorced." And together the two mothers took steps.

According to Mother, when Bob arrived home from work the next afternoon, Garnett's mother was sitting in the living room on the flowered couch with the fluffy goose-down cushions. She withdrew a revolver from her handbag, pointed it at Bob, and told him if he ever saw her daughter again she would kill him.

"That afternoon this episode in our life ended," Mother wrote. "I never referred to it again but this was the beginning of a deepening hurt around which I built a shell without being conscious of the building." So, on April 2, 1940, "Katie Bob was born. Her christened name was Katherine after my German Aunt Kate and

Roberta after [her] father of whom she was the spittin' image. Dr. Matt Garrad said, 'She is as pretty as a speckled pup.' . . . Her eyes were almost larger than her face and later to turn a dark brown." Life was smoother for a while after my arrival, and Cat became pregnant again in 1942. My younger brother, Richard Miller Bateman, was born on January 1, 1943.

During these years Catharine's relationship with Wynemah improved as well. They'd learned how to live with one another despite their differences, and Wynemah had even come to tolerate Bob in a distant, but quick to distrust, way.

In February 1944 Bob joined the Marine Corps. Catharine's writings indicate her resentment. She did not know that Bob was following a family pattern. Every male in the family, since the Backenstoes came over, had fought to protect the country. Even Bob's father had been a member of the Ohio National Guard during a span of relative peace in America and had served with distinction in the Spanish-American War.

Bob went off to Camp Pendleton in southern California, and in a few months we followed. Dick was one, and I was four. Besides the two of us, Catharine had fourteen pieces of luggage, which held not only clothes but the accoutrements to make a tasteful home—even if it was in a quickly built row hut for military families. Catharine described this period as "a nine-month period of apprehensive happiness."

Even though I was only four and five during those years, I remember our family being happy during that year in California—the trips to the beach, the affection between my mother and father, Dick toddling here and there. The Millers were there as well. Aunt Ada and Uncle Hi had moved to La Jolla around 1940 following Horace's retirement from Armco Steel and his stint as mayor of Middletown. I can still remember napping on a daybed in the sitting room and dozing off to the sound of the ocean, which was visible from every window in the house.

Then Bob was off to Hawaii and Japan, and Catharine returned to her dream house in Old Orchard. She was happy to be back and happy for another reason. War had changed her husband, now "a lonesome man far from home and family, a family he was accepting for the first time as the most important part of his existence." Love letters arrived weekly—letters that have passed down to me. I can remember Catharine's pleasure when Bob's letters arrived, and I remember her writing Bob at her dressing table in front of the bedroom window. If I did not interrupt her she would let me look in her dressing table drawer until I found the tiny white box that I was searching for, a jeweler's box that was my only connection to my dead older brother. In the prim little cube was a delicate gold cross on a wisp of a chain and a dried rose bud that came from his grave. "Tell me again about Bobby Junior," I would ask Mother. And she would reply the same each time, "You had a brother who died before you were born. He was named after Daddy just like you."

For years before the war my father had been a lay reader in the Calvary Episcopal Church in Ashland. The war changed Bob even more than Catharine realized. When he returned from Japan in November 1945 he told her he wanted to be an Episcopal minister. He was given a small mission church, St. John's, in Corbin, Kentucky. Catharine was heartsick. She moved the family "with a great amount of resentment. Corbin was a dirty railroad center bisected by a small odorous creek. The rectory . . . was barely a shell with a tin roof that held the heat of the sun in the summer and was an escape route for the heat in the winter." Her description of life in Corbin drips with sarcasm: "The children and I went to church every day while Father Bateman, as he was now called, practiced droning morning prayer to a captive congregation of three."

Signs of the impending divorce between my parents show up in Mother's journal entries from 1947. There is the constant, draining service to the church, with little emotional return, Catharine's distaste for the rectory, the growing tightness of money, and Bob's drinking, which was becoming a problem again. Finally, she wrote in her 1980 account, it "dawned on me that I did not have to live the rest of my life being exploited by everybody including God. . . . I picked up my children, packed up our clothes, and on January 1, 1949 I was on my way to 3830 Thornwell Road."

That day marks one of the most painful events of my life—and of my brother's and perhaps of Catharine's. It was Dick's sixth birthday. I was eight. Mother picked us up after our regular Sunday movie matinee. I was confused since it was always Daddy who came. Then instead of going home for Dick's birthday cake, we went to our fellow parishioners the Gilispies' house, where our packed clothes were already waiting. Then something went wrong. There was yelling. Mother was standing in the open heavy wooden doorway. Daddy was there too. They were angry. Mother slammed the door and locked it. I had never seen my parents fight. I'd known tension, but I had never heard yelling.

Frances Gilispie had a cake for Dick. But as we lit the candles, a loud popping noise came from outside. Daddy—the former revenue man and star marksman—was shooting into the house. Burt Gilispie wrapped an arm around each of us—Dick and me—and sat with us there in the dark in his deepest leather chair. He made soothing sounds, telling us that we would be OK, that he would keep us safe.

The police came and took Daddy home. We slept in the help's rooms on the third floor in case Bob returned with his gun. On the third floor "a bullet would only hit the ceiling," Mother said. The next morning we stepped on the train in Corbin and stepped off in Ashland to Wynemah's wringing hands.

Dick's and my life with our father ended abruptly that January 1—the day we should have been celebrating Dick's birthday. Bob remarried shortly after his divorce from Catharine and started a new family. I was ten the next time I saw him. By then I had a baby half-sister, born May 2, 1950, exactly ten years and one month after my birth. They were living in Covington, Kentucky, at the time. But then he and his second family—my half-sister, then half-brother, and finally my baby half-sister—were sent to an Episcopal parish in Libertyville, Illinois, then to Montana, and finally to Nevada, where they stayed. I was with Bob only ten days before he died at age sixty-five.

Catharine chose the painful time after the breakup of her marriage to take her "year upstairs." Unlike her beloved "Gram," who had felt safest in her bedroom, where she could read and sip bourbon in front of the sunny window looking out on the Congregational Church across the street, Catharine felt safest with her "Auntie." She took Dick and moved to the shelter of Lena's arms and the flamingo pink walls of her home in Coral Gables, Florida. She left me with Wendell and Wynemah. That year Catharine was gone I became—and would emotionally remain—my grandmother's child. Until her death Wynemah's stories and mine would be intertwined, and together we would reenact the family patterns.

13

GRANDDAUGHTERS

WYNEMAH **MOTT** Meinhart was the granddaughter of Kizzie Clay Burns, who refused to return to her fine house in Prestonsburg after Garfield took it over because "it would never be clean again." Kizzie Clay was the granddaughter of Phoebe Belcher Clay, who helplessly watched the killing and scalping of two of her children and learned later of the torturous death of a third. Phoebe Belcher Clay was the granddaughter of Mary Mitchell Clay, who lied under oath to protect the Clay family honor.

Catharine Meinhart Bateman was the granddaughter of Kate Burns Mott, who was the first to "go upstairs" for a year. Kate Burns Mott was the granddaughter of Rebecca Cecil Clay, who said "you cannot make a silk purse out of a sow's ear" and who expected to be treated like a member of Elizabeth I's court. Rebecca Cecil Clay was the granddaughter of Elizabeth Cecil Witten, who was also her great-aunt. Rebecca Cecil Clay was also the great-great-great-great-great-great-granddaughter of

William Cecil, Lord Burghley—the only relative that really mattered to her if the stories are true.

I am the granddaughter of them all. But first, and foremost, I am Wynemah's granddaughter. She took over when Mother spent her year in Coral Gables. She provided a safe place for me to forget my confusion and my fear. She told me family stories and began to prepare me to "be strong like all the rest." And then, even after she disclosed to Mother my secret request for adoption after I had lived with her for a year, and even after Mother came and took me away when I was ten, I was still my grandmother's child.

When Mother returned from Florida she moved back to her "dream house" on the edge of Ashland. Soon, however, she found she could not manage the job as a bookkeeper she took to support Dick and me and take care of us without help. When she learned from Wynemah that the house directly across the street from Wynemah and Wendell was about to go on the market, she sold her beloved house at 3830 Thornwell Road and moved. Once again she was back under her mother's watchful eye. Once again Wynemah was in control, just as she had been when she enticed Catharine and her young husband Frederick to live at home two decades earlier.

Catharine's new house was nothing like the white clapboard Cape Cod cottage she left behind. It had been constructed in the 1920s of dark brown brick. A deep heavy-lidded porch stretched across the front. Instead of sitting on a rise that stretched into the sunny fields of wildflowers of Old Orchard, this house nestled into a steep hillside in a niche that had been leveled out just for it. There was a side yard with room for a cherry tree and Mother's compost heap and a shallow backyard with a clothesline. The rest of the property was just hillside—wild vines, redbuds, and dogwoods in the back and grass in front that had to be cut with a lawn mower tied to a rope that controlled the roll down the steep slope to the brick street below. Three flights of stairs led up to the porch—stairs that started almost directly across the street from Wendell and Wynemah's front porch where they often sat on summer evenings.

For Dick and me the move was a godsend. Though we were now without our father, Wendell and Wynemah provided us with a safe haven, a structure, a known environment. We picked up our lunches at their house on the way to school and returned for snacks on the way home. We learned to play cards at Wynemah's cherry card table with the magic swivel top that hid the cards, coasters, and score sheets—the same table that serves as one of my desks in my study now. And each weekday evening at six o'clock on the dot Dick and I practiced a family ritual: we rode with Wynemah to pick up Granddaddy at the Elks Club.

The routine was always the same. We scrambled out of the car as soon as Wynemah pulled to the curb. We bounded up the thirty-six steep steps to see who would win the race to the top, to see who would first get to stand under the Roman portico with its tall columns and look for nesting sparrows. Then we would debate over whose turn it was to stretch up and push the brass bell by the giant glass door to the large foyer where the lifelike elk peered down at us while we waited. After the push of the bell we could see Al the doorman round the corner from the mysterious room in the back and start his slow agonizing hobble down the endless hall to let us in.

Once we got inside Dick hopped and tap danced on the dark granite floors as he moved with Al toward the back. I, however, walked with sedate delight past the ballrooms on either side—ballrooms decorated with gleaming brass sconces and heavy crown moldings and chandeliers of dripping crystals. I often paused in one of the wide pocket doorways to admire the black-lacquered grand piano with its lid propped at an angle. And sometimes I gingerly stepped on the thick oriental carpets that could be rolled up for dances—dances that I could envision clearly from Wynemah's stories long before I was allowed to go up the Elks steep steps alone, stories about flirtatious Saturday nights my grandparents spent with friends on weekends when they were young.

Finally, at the end of the hall—out of sight from the glass front door—was the most magic part of our six o'clock ritual. On Al's desk sat a baffling black box with a grilled front and a lever on one side. Al would grin at us, then put his face close to the grill, raise the lever, and shout, "Meiney, the kids are here!" Over the raucous deep din that surged out of that box the minute the lever was lifted came the familiar "Yo!" And soon our dear, round German grandfather would lumber up the steps in a stale cloak of cigarette smoke and put a hand on each of our heads, and we would walk back down the long hall and down the steep steps to Wynemah, who was all made up for Wendell in one of her voile dresses and with her iron-gray curls wisping out of the silver-studded combs despite her constant battle to control them. We were safe—Dick and I—in our skipped-generation family of four.

Life with Catharine was another story. Catharine had not returned to Ashland alone. Her Corbin friend Frances Gilispie— who had divorced her husband while Catharine was in Florida— came with her. Like Bob, Frances was an alcoholic. This time, however, Catharine did not mark in her diary the number of drinks Frances had each evening as she had done with Bob. This time Catharine drank with her. Although Mother had told me that she left Daddy because he was an alcoholic, I had never seen him altered, had never seen him drunk. Now, although Frances had her own apartment a few blocks away, I was confronted with drunkenness most nights.

I was appalled and angry. Finally, one Saturday morning when Mother was too sick to get out of bed, she asked me to help her. I replied, "You got yourself into this, you get yourself out," and I left her in her room, walked out the front door, down the steep steps, and crossed the street to the safety of my grandparents' house. But there was no escape. Wynemah had plans for me. Tired of being solely responsible for her only child, my grandmother passed Catharine on to me. I can remember clearly the day that Wynemah informed me of my new role. It was a Saturday morning, and she and I had just finished our special treat of toast fried crisp in bacon grease topped with raspberry jelly from Wynemah's precious homemade supply. We were sitting at the cherry drop-leaf breakfast table by the kitchen window—the same window that a few months later would let the light stream across the kitchen toward the red glass fairy balls while I learned of Lena's syphilitic sore. Mother had recently been in the hospital, diagnosed with a heart condition, according to Wynemah. After we finished our toast and jelly Wynemah looked at me with that blatant black eyed gaze of hers and declared, "You must take care of your mother or she will die. And you know what that means. You will have to go live with that god-damned bastard your father."

I was eleven that year Wynemah gave Catharine to me—the same age that Wynemah was the year her mother "went upstairs." My first thought was that I might someday again get to live with my father, whom I had never ceased missing. But immediately the guilt rushed in: in order to live with Daddy, Mother had to die. That moment changed my life. Not only did I become my mother's keeper, I excelled at my job. Only when Catharine died at age ninety was I freed from caring for and trying—unsuccessfully—to fix her alcoholism.

Wynemah had trained me well for my assignment. She had begun to teach me housekeeping skills the year Mother lived with Lena in Coral Gables. She continued with vigor when we moved across the street. She showed me how to bring dish towels to a slow lye-soap boil on her basement stove and then how to stir them with the broken handle of an old broom. She taught me how to let the sun bleach stains out of snow-white linens too delicate for the lye boil and how to wash the winter dirt out of oriental carpets. She taught me how to dust furniture and polish silver. She told me how she organized her time, how she kept a running list of special projects for Eddie—her handyman—to do each week. She showed me how she put her unpaid bills in a particular cubbyhole in her walnut slant-top desk and then shifted them to another when they were paid. She taught me how to organize my time so that I could take care of the house and still participate in after-school activities, just as she did with her bridge club and church circle events.

Catharine thrived under my care. No more hospital stays, no signs of heart distress. I learned how to manage the house and school and the part-time job in a small printing company that I took on when I was fifteen. The drinking continued, but guilt outweighed my revulsion and Mother's "peace at any cost" motto became Dick's and my motto as well.

When it was time to go to college I thought I should not leave—could not possibly leave Mother to fend for herself—but she assured me she would be fine and hired a cleaning lady and a laundress. College for me was one of the happiest and most carefree periods of my life. I had no one to take care of except myself, and I was out from under the tug-of-war between Catharine and Wynemah for my affection.

Years later I asked Mother about that period in her life when I became her caretaker. I was on one of my twice-yearly visits to Kentucky. She was drinking iced tea and telling me how well her annual doctor's visit had gone, which caused me to ask, "Mother, what was wrong with your heart when I was young?" She looked puzzled and said, "What do you mean?" I said, "You know. When you were in the hospital so often, and then you couldn't walk upstairs or carry groceries and you needed me to do all the house-keeping and the laundry." She said, "There was never anything wrong with my heart. I don't know what you are talking about." "But Meme [my name for Wynemah] told me there was something wrong with your heart, and if I didn't take care of you, you would die." She chortled. "That sounds just like Mother," she said. While Mother had been in and out of the hospital, treated for appendicitis, pneumonia, and phlebitis, she'd never had a heart condition.

I made it to my bedroom. Leaning against the edge of the cherry cannonball bed that I still think of as my mother and father's bed, I cried in shock and anger. Anger at the two women who had deceived me. Anger at my grandmother for giving my mother to me. Anger at my mother for allowing my childhood to be used up taking care of her, anger that she had expected to be taken care of just as she had been as an only child. I had been betrayed. Mother and I never spoke of the betrayal. It was not our pattern to confront issues. It was instead our pattern to pretend certain conversations had not occurred, certain declarations had never been voiced. It was by then too late to confront Wynemah—who would have denied any part of the charade had she still been alive.

I—who rarely cry and then primarily in anger—cried off and on throughout the next day. A year or so later I came across a reference to a practice said to be especially prevalent in Southern families. According to the author, it was common in the South for grandmothers to pass on the caretaking of their adult daughters to their granddaughters. So there it was. It was not just my story. It was one I have shared with other granddaughters without knowing it.

Despite Wynemah's machinations, I knew she loved me. Unlike Mother, I was neither afraid of Wynemah's temper nor guilt-ridden by her common complaint that "no one appreciates me." I know that she, like her mother, Kate, was a better grandmother than she was a mother. According to Mother she was less mercurial as I was growing up than she had been when Mother was small. Still, she would fly into a rage at times that could shake the family peace. Some of those times I would stand and fight, tell her that her charges were incorrect, unfair. Mother would implore me not to argue with her, not to make it worse, but I was not Mother. Underneath my quiet, even-natured exterior I was Wynemah's child. Instead of filling me with trembling, shrinking fear as she had done to her daughter, she had instilled in me a tensile strength, her strength. I did not take her anger personally.

I took my clue from my German grandfather, who had stayed with Wynemah through the rough spots that began in their courtship and continued through a marriage of decades. I have known always that Wendell was as much of a lifeline for me after my parents' divorce as Wynemah. She gave me strength. He gave me calm. When I moved into my grandparents' house I'd slipped from my father's lap into his.

And then my beloved grandfather was gone. His heart had been weakening throughout his sixties and early seventies. In

1962 at age seventy-six it finally gave out. I was in graduate school in Ann Arbor at the time. I had married a fellow student at Berea at the end of my senior year, and we had headed to the University of Michigan to do our graduate work. Dick was a sophomore at Berea College by then, majoring in music, and it was he who went back to Ashland from Berea to be with Granddaddy the last few days of his life. As arranged, I flew down from Ann Arbor to be with Catharine and Wynemah during the funeral.

There is a funny and telling story about my grandmother that occurred between Wendell's death and his funeral. According to Mother, Wynemah felt remorse immediately after Wendell died. She repeatedly said that she had been a terrible wife, that she had had affairs, that she had not been kind to him, that he had been the most loving partner in the marriage. Mother finally got tired of hearing the ranting and raving and told Wynemah something she had withheld from her for years. One night when Catharine was in her late twenties and returning home from a late bridge game, she disclosed, she'd seen her father's car parked in front of the house of a divorcee with a questionable reputation. She'd pulled over, parked, and walked straight into the house. (Nobody locked their doors in Ashland except Wynemah, who slept with a handgun in her bedside table drawer.) Wendell was comfortably ensconced on the sofa with a drink in his hand. Mother had told him to leave immediately and that if she ever saw his car there again or heard he had been there she would "tell Mother." He'd kept his part of the bargain, and so had she—until now, when Wynemah was filled with guilt over her own love affairs. Wynemah's response to the disclosure, as the story goes, was predictable: "Why, that god-damned bastard! I should have left him years ago when I had the chance!" And her indignation got her through this difficult period in her life.

Nine months after Wendell's death, my brother Dick died in an automobile accident. He was nineteen. He had left college before his junior year to join the Marine Corps as Bob had done twenty years before. It was 1963, just before the Vietnam years. Dick did not know when he enlisted that each of his male relatives on our father's side had been soldiers. Each Bateman, Bell, and Backenstoe male had prided himself on his military endeavors, had passed on to his son stories about fighting the British for independence, the French and the Indians and the Spanish for land, his own countrymen for cohesion, and on and on and on. He did not know that each Bateman male had hung framed papers of commendation, had carefully saved his ribbons and medals in velvet boxes and kept them in a special place.

Dick was home on leave when the accident occurred. He had just finished his basic training and had been accepted for parachute training. He was happy. I was happy for him and was preparing for his trip to Ann Arbor the next week. Instead of his visit I got a call in the middle of the night. It was Mother yelling hysterically, "He's dead! Dick's dead! Come home. Don't drive!" I vomited on the side of the road the length of Ohio on my way back to Ashland. Dick had been my link to laughter, to silliness, to openness. I did not guard what I said with him. I did not hide. He was my brother. I did not have to impress, or be nice, or act smart or not act smart. I was just "Sis." And now I was alone, an only child with two dead brothers.

Nine months after Dick died, Wynemah complained about a painful headache, but she always complained about something hurting so no one really listened. The next day she was in the hospital, diagnosed with an inoperable brain tumor. Wynemah got lost once while in the hospital. She climbed over the railings of her bed and wandered off. It took several hours before the hospital staff found her in the main linen closet, straightening all the clean sheets and pillowcases so that they were neatly turned with the smooth curve out—the way she had taught me to store my freshly ironed linens. Somehow escaping and folding linens made her illness easier. It made a good story, a perfect Wynemah story.

I went home to help out Mother the weekend before Wynemah died—not knowing it would be quite so soon. I was five months pregnant with my first child, and I stood by my grandmother's bed in Mother's most recent house, Century House, and put Wynemah's hand on my stomach. I told her I was going to have a baby, could she feel the baby move? Although she was beyond knowing, I needed her to bless my first child by her touch. She died in her sleep that night, February 29, 1964.

I was twenty-three when my family vanished. Over a period of eighteen months I became a granddaughter without grand-parents, a sister without a brother to share my sadness. It was just Mother and me. Each of us would have preferred to be left with any of the others instead of alone with each other. But then that is something we could never talk about—even if Mother and I were able to talk about things of consequence. She did speak of that terrible period of death later—one time when bourbon had loosened her tongue. She said that I was cold, that I had not even hugged her "when Daddy died." I did not think it worth reminding her that the first time I came home from college I had gone up behind her in a surge of affection and hugged her while she stood at the kitchen sink. Then I told her I loved her. She shrugged me off and over her shoulder said, "Oh Katie, you know I don't like that sort of thing."

14

HOUSE LUST

*I*F YOU are receptive, houses will speak to you. I learned it from Century House, the house that Mother bought and named in 1957, the year I left for college, a house that resonates inside me still. Century House was a tall brick antebellum house built on an original land grant in 1850 in Catlettsburg, Kentucky. Catlettsburg—where the Big Sandy River flowed into the Ohio—adjoined Ashland along their river frontage. It was there in Catlettsburg that John Burns moved Kizzie Clay in 1864, where she died holding his hand despite his long affair and eventual marriage to Josephine Chrisman. Kate Burns met Frank Mott in Catlettsburg and bore the three beauties and the Crown Prince in a house near the river. Century House sat across the street from the courthouse where John Burns had reigned as judge—the courthouse the family called "John Burns's Courthouse." And it was next door to Kizzie's fine Catlettsburg house, had it still been standing. Perhaps this is why Mother had to buy that house, for indeed she said she "had to have it."

At Century House thick Doric columns stretched up two high stories to support a Greek-temple gable at the top and a wide upstairs veranda on the way. On hot summer nights Mother, Dick, and I would sit out there trying to read while moths swooped here and there in their claim for a share of the dim yellow glow of the porch lamp. I loved that veranda that once overlooked the wide Ohio River before small-town growth got in the way. I loved it not only for the cool evening breezes while we waited for the daytime heat to leak out of the house; I loved it because I could picture the races—the races I knew from the guest book that each previous owner had left with the house, the guest book that chronicled the hundred-plus years of visitors and their activities.

The guest book was a magic document to me. Within its hard-worn leather covers were the signatures and notes of those who had visited the house during the Civil War, notes of both Union and Confederate soldiers, notes of relatives and friends. The visitors wrote about the races from the porch to the river and back. When I held that embossed leather book, with its horizontal layout and wide flowery scripts that scurried across the pages, I could see the soldiers in their blue or gray uniforms and hear the laughter of the girls in their frilly hooped skirts, girls trying to be the first up the curving central stairs to the veranda, the first to stand by the rail and cheer on a sweetheart or a brother or a cousin.

Even though Kentucky had remained neutral during the War and even though only the Ohio River divided Catlettsburg from the North, Century House could have been the Deep South stage set for Tara or Twelve Oaks. On either side of the wide entrance hall that ran from front to back of the house were double drawing rooms sixteen feet square with twelve-foot-high ceilings. Casement doors between the rooms allowed the spaces to be free-flowing or intimate. Either way, deep crown molding, graceful fireplaces, and foot-deep windowsills added a quiet elegance. Every room in the house had shutters. Each summer morning—in repetition of southern habits for centuries—I closed the shutters, slanting them just right to entrap the cooler night air but still allow a bit of light. And each time I did this, without fail, I would imagine Scarlet O'Hara peeking through the shutters in Atlanta as Sherman's troops swarmed in.

Large oil portraits of Uncle Harry Wood's dour grandmother and prosperous grandfather hung in deep gilded frames over the fireplaces in the double drawing rooms. Kizzie Clay's couch, upholstered by then in rich salmon-colored brocade, sat at one end of the room facing the Haitian daybed—once at Wellesley—thirty-two feet away. Antique Persian rugs centered each space and gave scale to the various chairs and side tables dotting the rooms. On the other side of the hall behind the dining room and the "everyday sitting room," as Mother called our less formal living room, was a large kitchen with a massive fireplace. On winter breaks I would join Mother and Dick in the heavy black rocking chairs that had once graced the front porch of Kate Burns's "elegant gem of small-town splendor" but now circled the raised brick hearth. We would sit there with feet propped toward the warmth of the fire. Through the back door and off a long enclosed wooden porch was the yard with Mother's flower and vegetable gardens plus a famous apple tree that produced three varieties of apples, three trees grafted together by the home's original owner. Behind that was the former slave quarters, a two-story frame building that was a grave embarrassment to me.

Upstairs the floor plan was the same as below—four large bedrooms with fireplaces, one on each corner off a wide central hall with stairs continuing their curve up to a third floor, which was full of small rooms with low ceilings. Above the kitchen, which had been added onto the back, was a large bathroom with the original tub on articulated lion's feet. The tub sat at right angles to the fireplace so that you could lean back against that perfect old-tub slope and gaze into the fire. The bathroom—separated from the toilet, which had its own room—was a magic place.

My bedroom, on the front of the house, had a history. The corner of the room had been hit by lightning twice decades earlier, and each time a huge wedge of the house's foot-thick wall had been chewed out in an instant. I was always aware of those lightning strikes. I was more disconcerted, however, by the bats that sometimes dropped down the chimney in my room as evening fell. Some nights I slept with my head under the covers. Other times, when I knew a bat was in my room, I would sit on Captain Peter Hurd's sea chest just outside my bedroom door. I could read in the dim light of the upstairs chandelier and wait for the errant bat to find the velvet curtains that at night covered the leaded-glass sidelights and door to the veranda. The bats loved those curtains. Perhaps it was their burgundy color or maybe it was the sturdiness of the heavy velvet, which hung in deep folds from the thick wooden rod above the door. All I know is that once a bat left my bedroom it would invariably head toward the curtains and hang in their musty, dark folds until morning, when one of us would stun it with a broom and release it outside.

Century House taught me that houses have souls. I learned that memories linger in walls and shutters and hover in high ceiling corners. I also learned that houses remain neutral, collecting all events whether good or bad and releasing them randomly. I did not need the record of the guests who came to Mother's house on the slight rise above the Ohio River to know that houses could induce magic.

Mother sold Century House two years after our family disintegrated. She could not stand her recollections of Dick, which shadowed her as she walked through those spacious elegant rooms. She left Catlettsburg and Ashland—with all the family connections—and moved to central Kentucky, to Berea, where she had been offered a job with the college. She had always been a bookkeeper, except during her early years as mother and preacher's wife, and had loved the detective game of making debits and credits end up properly on the bottom line. At Berea College she worked with students rather than numbers and thrived with new friends and experiences.

In 1970 my husband and I accepted positions at Berea College. After nine years of working on our doctorates in Ann Arbor and having three young children, we returned to the place where we had met. Those were good years for Mother and me; we were in a good place with each other. I had returned to Kentucky, as she had hoped I would, and she was drinking in moderation, a dream of mine. We were each happy in our lives.

Mother formed close friendships in Berea based on common intellectual interests rather than on multigenerational family ties. She joined book clubs. She became a leader in the college-supported church. She retired and provided my three children with a multitude of stories that they could tell their children about hiking, frog hunting, cookie making, overnights with ghost stories, toasted marshmallows, and popcorn by the fire. She relished her time with her grandchildren, as they did with her. She, like the other Clay and Cecil mothers, was a better grandmother than a mother.

But then the easy relationship Mother and I had finally built together ended. I did something that embarrassed her, caused her to have to make excuses for me, made her feel that she had to explain to the college community that we were both such a part of why I did what I did. Thirteen years after I married my first husband, I fell deeply in love with a sculptor who taught in my department. We divorced our current spouses and married each other. And then I did an unthinkable thing for the early 1970s: I became the noncustodial parent of my children. I moved out of my solid chestnut house on the side of a hill with a view of the mountains—a house considered by many to be "one of the finest houses in town." I left the family furniture, the silver, and the dishes. I took my clothes, my typewriter, and my art history library and moved to a tiny house two blocks away—close enough for the children to stop by on their way home from school—and I started over.

There was no joint custody in those days. The children's father had a tenure-track position in the physics department. I was not on a tenure track. I was afraid I would not be able to support the house we had purchased to raise the children—a house that had seemed to us perfect for each stage of their school life. Because of these things I made the decision—in conjunction with the children's father—to be the one who moved out and voluntarily paid child support as he would have been forced to do had he been the one who left.

I wonder now—and have for some years—if I was destined to live out a family story. Despite the careful logic behind the hardest decision I ever made in my life—a decision that took years to come to terms with—I wonder if I was taking my turn at "a year upstairs," just as Kate Burns did when Wynemah was eleven and as Mother did when I was eight. I will never know for sure, but as I look back at my family history, it gives me pause. Did the family stories propose an option that others would not have considered in the early 1970s in a small, tightly knit college town in Kentucky?

Fifteen years after Mother moved to Berea, she moved back to Ashland to marry my stepfather, Silas William "Bill" Hearne. They were each sixty-nine and had been neighbors when Dick and I and his two sons were young. She moved into his large house on a hill that overlooked her previous homes—her parents', the year with Frederick, and the "dream house" years with Bob. She renewed her old childhood friendships, and eventually alcohol crept back into her life. Wynemah had quit drinking in her early forties. Throughout my childhood she would say to me, with her gnarled knuckles spread and curled into falcon's talons to accentuate her point, "Stay away from alcohol. Before you know it, it will get you in its clutches." I think we both knew it was too late for Mother.

Two years after my divorce I was hired away from Berea College by The School of the Art Institute of Chicago to teach in their art history department. My sculptor husband—who also had been promised a job—and I moved to Chicago. The children spent the summers and holidays with us and the school year in Berea. Then, one by one they joined me full-time in Illinois. We are now a family of the Midwest—colleges, spouses, jobs—yet all of us are rooted in Kentucky.

And so on a cold, drizzly weekend in March 1999 I visited Kentucky. I went with a childhood friend, Alan, who had filled in the spaces of Mother's life, spaces created by Dick's death and my desire to escape the encumbrances of the Kentucky stories. Alan had been the good child throughout our growing-up years, the one who did not complain when Mother tried something new and stylish for our Christmas tree, the one who could enjoy a sip of bourbon with her by the fire. He had been the one who went antiquing with Catharine, who learned from her how to identify woods by spitting on a finger and rubbing an unpainted spot and how to refinish potentially priceless pieces. He was the one who shared with her the love of the chase, who relished the unexpected find.

So there we were, two lifelong friends—"second-grade sweethearts," Alan called us—driving along narrow central Kentucky roads I knew by heart even after years of living away. Low dry-stacked limestone walls still confined the narrow lanes as did the white wooden fences that meandered out in front of us in curves and curls following the original Indian hunting trails. The mares in the pastures searched for tender tufts of early bluegrass, round and plush with winter fur and the racehorse champions they carried. We were heading toward Mount Sterling, a small town on the edge of the Bluegrass region, a town Alan wanted me to see, a town that had hardly changed since we drove through it on our shared rides back to Ashland from our two colleges nearby. Without that fancy of his about Mount Sterling this book might not have been written, for that afternoon in that tiny town on the edge of the Bluegrass region I saw a house that touched something deep inside me, and I bought it on the spot.

I had not been to Kentucky since Mother's death fifteen months earlier. She had died in the den of her big house with her hospital bed facing her spring garden. It was too early for Reddy Red Bird, her favorite cardinal, to show off his new family, but I talked to her in her coma about him—reminding her that he would peck on her bedroom window if she did not put food out for him before his morning visit. I talked about her flower beds and her big vegetable garden—the garden that grew railroad-tie square by square year after year. I reminded her of her delicious warm and juicy tomatoes that she loved to eat for breakfast and the slender green beans she would pick one by one off the vines until she had a handful, just enough for supper. I remembered out loud how the seeds from the huge heads of dill she planted one spring blew everywhere until she finally had to wrench her garden back from its all-consuming growth.

I told her how lovely the huge silver cedars that surrounded the house looked with a skiff of snow barely hanging onto the lacy edges of the swooping swags that swayed ever so slightly in the nighttime breeze. Each evening as she lay there in her hospital bed, I told her that I had turned on the lamps near the windows in the living room and the front hall just as she did on winter nights to make the house look inviting despite its stately presence there on the rise overlooking Old Orchard. And I told her how I sometimes stepped outside and looked toward Wendell and Wynemah's former house—the one where she and Frederick lived during the mistake of their short marriage, but I didn't mention that. And then I told her how I would turn and look the other way toward 3830 Thornwell Road, her "dream house," where Dick and I were born and where she and Bob had such happy and unhappy times. I said that it must have been nice for her to survey her life from there on the rise after she married that one last time, after she married my dear, stable stepfather who gave her financial security and undivided love.

I talked to her about all the things I wished I had been able to say to her when we were younger. I told her that it had been hard for me to share her with alcohol but that I never ceased loving her. I told her how appreciative I was for all the good traits I inherited from her—her brightness, her charisma, her personal ease—and I said that she was not to worry about me. I told her I was financially comfortable and I was able to take care of myself—that I had listened when she told me to always have my own money, to not count on a man to take care of me. And I stroked her hair and put my face close to her cheek and kissed and held her still-lovely hands with their tapered fingers and shapely nails like Wendell's, and like mine. And I dozed with my head next to hers on her pillow. For ten days and nights I did those things—those things that showed love, those things she had not taught me—until she finally let go. She had lived to the age she had set for herself, ninety, just months past the age her grandmother Kate Burns was when she died. I had gone to Kentucky to celebrate Mother's ninetieth birthday two months before she died. When I tucked her into bed that birthday night she said with a proud smile, "I've lived as long as Gram."

When she died I was dazed. I had acted as her mother, but she had also been mine. Now I was truly orphaned, and Dick was not there to share the grief. So I grieved alone and I grieved for them all. I grieved for the loss of Wendell and Wynemah, for Catharine and Bob, and I grieved for my dead brothers, Dick and Bobby Junior—the younger brother with whom I had shared my youth and the older brother who was there and yet not there.

I closed up the house, split the family antiques among my children, and dug up cold clumps of Mother's primroses to take back to Chicago. I went to the cemetery and stood by the graves of my brothers buried on either side of Wendell—the sons Wynemah denied him. I walked to Mother's mausoleum where she had chosen an outside spot that faced her mother's burial site in an adjoining mausoleum. And I walked the short distance to that older mausoleum to look at my grandmother's marker and that of my great-grandmother Kate directly across the shadowed nave from her daughter and her mother Kizzie Clay, and I left Kentucky with no reason to return—until a house pulled me back.

15

KENTUCKY MY WAY

Kentucky's terrain rolls gently up toward Mount Sterling—from the deep limestone cut of the Kentucky River to the west, past Frankfort, the state capital, and Lexington, the heart of the Bluegrass region. Before Mount Sterling comes into view, the mountains do. Not the peaked barren-topped mountains of the western United States. Rather mountains with rounded comforting silhouettes. Mountains clothed in cedars and pines, each spring giving way to dogwoods that cascade down the slopes in horizontal waves of creamy white and rich red mixed with the soft rose wisps of redbuds.

These mountains are mine. I know the quality of the light, the softness of the air. I know them in a nonverbal way, from inside out. The earliest memory I can recall is from my sunsuit years. I must have been close to two. Although I had no words to describe it then, the image is full-blown. I am looking out the front screen door of Mother's dream house on the rise in Old Orchard. The narrow valley and the back road to Catlettsburg begin there at the foot of our hill. The screen is rough but I like the feeling as I trace the road that curls back and forth like a snake. I can feel the warmth of the sun on my stomach. I can smell the summer, the grass, the bushes outside, the flowers on the table. I am wrapped in the safety of my home in Kentucky.

When Alan and I drove into Mount Sterling I recalled why I had always liked that little town of five thousand so much. Little had changed from our college days. Eighteenth- and nineteenth-century brick and limestone buildings encircle the town square in front of the courthouse. The only "new" building on the square is the courthouse itself, twice destroyed by fire, once on purpose by the Confederates and once by accident.

Markers on the courthouse lawn and dotted around town tell of Civil War battles fought in Mount Sterling. The Union stronghold there was captured—along with mules, wagons, guns—won back, then lost, changing hands more than a dozen times during the course of the War. Near the courthouse and slightly up the hill is the Episcopal Church, which was originally a hospital for war casualties. Across the wide valley, crowning the top of the adjacent hill and in clear view from the former hospital windows, is a graveyard—a constant cue to fight for life.

A few yards up High Street and in a direct sight line from the cardinal-red doors of the Episcopal Church is a red brick house with steeply pitched gables. The house could be a church itself, for the wings of the house have sharply pointed roofs and tall, arched windows. It became my house, my Mount Sterling house, my return to Kentucky on my own terms. There is a story to tell about the purchase of the house, a story that is Kentucky at its heart.

Alan did not want to stop when I saw the For Sale sign in front of the house, but I made him back up so I could take a closer look. A wing jutted out beside the front door forming one of the porch walls. Victorian corbels supported the steeply pitched tin roof, which overhung a pair of tall arched windows structurally centered and classically defined by a carved limestone lintel with a keystone at the peak of its slow curve. High above the windows was a decorative oval vent accentuating the height of the roof's peak. Despite the cold drizzle I got out of the car and slowly circled the property.

A second wing, set somewhat back, jutted out at right angles to the first with its own pair of tall arched windows. As I walked around the house, I saw that each of the windows had the same gracious arch and limestone lintels. At the back of the house a final wing extended into the yard. As I rounded the back corner of the property, an L-shaped screened-in porch snuggled into two of the house's extensions.

The house was set on a large lot—three quarters of an acre, I found out later—that rose softly from front to back. There were trees of all types and sizes in the yard. One was more than fifty feet tall. The trunk, nearly eight feet in circumference, was encased in shiny leafed vines that provided a late winter nesting place for the dozens of birds that rustled in and out while I stood there in the rain. There was a tall spruce with deeply drooping boughs in the back corner of the yard that reminded me of the stately trees that surrounded Mother and Bill's house in Old Orchard. Dogwoods were everywhere, and slender redbuds.

I am not sure if it was the trees or the arched windows, the steep cathedral pitch of the roof or the screened-in porch. I only knew that I wanted that house with a deep longing. Against real estate etiquette and my longtime protection of individual privacy, I walked up the limestone steps onto the porch and knocked on the front door.

I had always been chagrined when Mother proudly told stories about knocking on strangers' doors during her rides through
the back roads of Kentucky in search of antiques. If she saw an
old rocking chair or a caned-seat side chair on a front porch, she
felt no compunction about walking onto the porch, calling out to
the owners, and asking if they had any furniture that they might
be willing to sell or trade. Each time I looked at the cherry corner
cupboard with its wavy bubbled glass in the upper doors—the
one she bought as soon as she married Frederick—I felt a twinge
of embarrassment. Catharine had talked an aging widower into
trading his family's kitchen cupboard for a new cabinet, which
she had delivered from the Ashland hardware store. When I saw
the house in Mount Sterling, I understood how she could do such
a thing.

No one answered my knock. I found a bed-and-breakfast
near the house to stay the one night I had left before I returned
to Chicago. I started making phone calls to try to get inside. I
phoned the listing agent, but she wasn't in so I left a message on
her machine. When she hadn't called by suppertime, I decided
to call the broker, Omar Prewitt, at home. He said the current
tenants required a twenty-four-hour notice. Perhaps since I was
from out of town they would make an exception. He would call
me back. He didn't. I called him again. The tenants were not at
home. I was to call him in the morning. The next morning his
wife said Omar was at church. I had to leave in four hours to
catch my plane. I asked what church he attended and went to find
him. Alan was beside himself. How did I know what he looked
like? How did I know where he parked? What was I thinking
of—buying a house in Kentucky when I lived in Chicago four
hundred miles away? All I could say was that I had to have the
house and that somehow I would find Omar.

Omar is a Baptist. The house I was determined to see inside was surrounded by Baptist church property. The house itself sat between the church and a large grassy area where church members parked. I miraculously had found a picture of Omar in a local chamber of commerce publication. I figured Omar would park in the church lot and walk past the house after the service to get to his car. So I stationed myself on the pitched limestone sidewalk by the For Sale sign and looked up from my postage stamp black-and-white photograph at each man walking out of the church heading toward his car. By the time I found Omar I had met several of his relatives. It was his cousin, in fact, who introduced us.

Omar is tall, boyishly handsome, and has never met a stranger. In good Kentucky fashion he hugged me hello, saying, "You must be Katherine." I told him about my rapidly decreasing time in Kentucky. He too broke real estate etiquette and marched up on the porch with his two small children in tow and knocked on the door. The tenants didn't answer. I returned to Chicago without going inside, but not without arranging for Alan, who lived in nearby Lexington, to go in for a viewing and describe to me what he saw.

Despite my desire to escape the family measures of worth, I inherited the house lust. I, like all the women in the family, loved houses. I loved the search, the daydreams, the anticipation. I loved to immerse myself in visual images of what this house or that might finally look like. I loved to design rooms, to plan kitchens, to knock down walls, to put up new ones. I could lose myself in templates of rooms and scaled-down furniture. For endless periods I could move tiny beds and couches, desks and chests and tables from room to room, switching them from this wall to that in the dollhouse I built in my mind. I loved every aspect of buying a house.

When Alan called after seeing the interior of the house, he said, "You won't believe the inside." Six days after I first found the house in Mount Sterling I had a signed contract. I learned later that my Kentucky background helped the house transactions move smoothly along. I also discovered—or rather Omar did by starting a conversation about Kentucky families—that he and I were distant cousins. He too was related to the first Henry Clay, the one who had fallen dead at the Clay family reunion in 1760. But there were many more connections to my family in Mount Sterling than I ever dreamed—connections I might have vaguely remembered but that did not surface during that first fateful afternoon trip.

On the April day of the closing, I paused for only a moment to gaze at dogwood trees ready to burst into snow white and ruby red blooms in the front yard. The force that compelled me to buy this house tugged me up the wide limestone walk toward the porch. It would be my first real look at the interior.

The women in our family have the ability to walk into a space and see it as it could be. Despite the fading wallpaper and some stains high on the walls from water leaks, the inside of my new house was breathtaking. There were twelve-foot-high ceilings throughout. All of the house's original woodwork was intact— deep baseboards and elaborate crown moldings, solid multipaneled shutters, double-hung doors. There were tasteful chandeliers in every room, even in the bathrooms, and fireplaces in the living room, dining room, and master bedroom.

That first time in late February, when I circled the perimeter of the house in the rain, I knew it had a peculiar layout for a late-Victorian-style home. When I stepped inside I realized how truly unique it was. The house was a house of vistas. It was laid out on one floor with wings extending in all directions. From every room numbers of other rooms were visible—from the living room you could look across the wide entrance hall into the master bedroom where the small Victorian fireplace with its delicately carved mantle was framed by the sculptured moldings of the bedroom door. If you shifted your stance slightly you could see past the creamy tones of the dining room into the cool pale green of the library.

The dining room was the central point in the house. From this room—nestled so neatly in the core of the house—you could enter the living room, the front hall, the library, the second bedroom, and, through a butler's door, walk a few steps down the back hall to the kitchen and pantry and the screened-in porch. Despite the number of doors in the dining room, it had a comfortable human-scale proportion. Pincapple-flocked wallpaper sheathed the walls—the only walls I did not paint. In the center of the high ceiling hung a chandelier with seven tiers of crystal pendants and—at the bottom—swags of sparkling beads that swooped between etched cups of soft light. A simple black marble fireplace matched the quiet elegance of the chandelier.

If the stories I soon learned about the house were true, none of the previous owners had wanted their tenure to end. As if in obeisance, each owner carefully cared for this house. The chimneys were cleaned each fall. The first sign of a leak caused heavy boots to clamber over the steep pitched roof in search of the culprit. Each owner dusted the stately woodwork and the fanciful tiles that surrounded the living room fireplace. Each polished the elegant chandeliers that graced the rooms, climbing high on ladders every spring and again in the fall. The hardwood floors were pampered with minute circles of wax applied with the softest cotton petticoats, especially in the long front hall where boards of mahogany alternated with maple to guide visitors to the sitting room or the library. The house was privileged. In return, it was kind to those who lived there. Although no guest book remained in the entrance hall like the one at Century House, the house rustled with history.

None of the memories were bad. There had been no mysterious deaths in these rooms, no unrequited loves, no strange lingering illnesses. No babies had died in the nursery next to the big bedroom. The influenza epidemic had not seeped under the solid shutters to wring the breath from the lungs of a mother or father. No one lost her mind here. There was nothing like that in this house.

This house was filled with love. It had been built as a wedding gift for a firstborn son of a wealthy German landowner in 1900. Joy flourished. In my imagination the newlyweds flounced from room to room not believing their good fortune to have such a house. Later the laughter of children slid off the walls and bounced across the oak floors until it reached the ears of their mother and lingered for a moment at the corners of her mouth.

As I got to know my house, a shadow would shimmer here or there, a flicker of movement on the edge of vision. A leaf might lift in a vase when there was no breeze. Sometimes I would catch a wisp of a sound, a phrase of a song, a few notes from a nonexistent piano. There would be a slight shudder in the floor as if someone just slipped out of the room. And during this time— this time back in Kentucky for a week each month—I began to remember the stories.

At first I thought I could not escape thinking about the Clays since Clay Street was just four doors away. I knew in an abstract way that Mount Sterling was in Clay country, but I had not thought about it at the time I purchased the house. Yet now I remembered that in the late eighteenth century Green Clay, Cassius Clay's father, had owned most of central Kentucky. I found myself wondering if I might be living on land once owned by him. Without thinking, I had thrust myself back into the history of my family, the family I had tried to escape by running to Ann Arbor and then to Chicago.

Then something happened. As the stories crept randomly back to consciousness I began to savor them. I started to jot down a bit of a story that Wynemah had told me, or something I remembered that Mother had said her "Gram" Kate Burns had told her about her grandmother Rebecca Cecil. As I walked through the rooms of my house the women in my family seemed to walk with me. Much of the family furniture once in Mother's house had been moved from Chicago back to Kentucky. Wynemah's Federal card table with the secret hiding place for cards and coasters was in Mount Sterling, as was Catharine's walnut washstand with the double doors that she loved so much. I used my grandmother's grape pattern silverware—the one she called her "everyday silverware"—and her stenciled brown plates and bowls. I hung up mirrors and etchings that had been Lena's at Wellesley and finally a year or so after the stories began to come back—I hung up the Clay family tree, something I had hidden in a back closet most of my life.

Soon after the stories began to resurface, I took a casual walk to Mount Sterling's library. I thought it might be fun to look for papers on the Clays. In the files I found references to John Thomas Claye and a copy of the epitaph on his father John Claye's tombstone in Wales. There were references to Cassius and his brothers and their father Green, and to the first Henry Clay, the grandfather of us all, but the collection in Mount Sterling was limited. Then I took the next step. I signed up as a scholar at the Newberry Library in Chicago and leaped into the historical search for my family. I made the decision to address my family in my own way—to research the Clays and the Cecils and the Burns and the Batemans just as I had researched medieval ivories and manuscripts years earlier.

I have recorded my search—my skepticism, my findings, the correlations with the storytellers' tales. The muddy boots in Kizzie Clay's house were real. Phoebe Belcher did lose three children in an Indian attack on their home, but there was more to the story than that: Liggon Blankenship saw what happened and left them all to die. Mary Mitchell perjured herself to protect the family honor, but no one told that story. What I have not yet related is something I discovered regarding two of my male relatives who spent time in Mount Sterling in 1862—one on the very land where my Mount Sterling house stands today, the other at the courthouse a block away.

Early on I described muster papers recording the volunteers for my great-grandfather Frank Mott's cavalry division during the Civil War. It sits under glass on my desk, as it did on Mother's desk before mine. One day while at my desk the words "Mount Sterling" jumped off the browning page of faded script: Frank Mott was headquartered in Mount Sterling in 1862. Historic markers dotted around the town tell the story. The Union soldiers hold Mount Sterling, the Confederate Army pushes them out, the Union battles back. Since my house sits on a high spot less than a block from the former military hospital, I feel comfortable with the knowledge that my great-grandfather Frank Mott and his fine white horse stood on my land under my giant tree a century and a half before I did.

John Mavity Burns was also in Mount Sterling in 1862. As I delved more deeply into documents regarding the Battle of Middle Creek, the one where Garfield requisitioned Kizzie Clay

Burn's fine house in Prestonsburg, I discovered where John Burns was when Kizzie and Roland were left alone in the house. He was in Mount Sterling attending the winter session of court. Eastern Kentuckians have long been known to hold a grudge for generations running, grudges often ending in pitched gun battles. At some point before the Civil War the Kentucky legislature determined to move major trials out of the mountains, away from potential danger to judge and jury. Mount Sterling was on the eastern edge of the Bluegrass region, with the foothills of the mountains visible in the distance. Further, the Old Pound Gap Road cut through the mountains straight from Prestonsburg—the political center of eastern Kentucky—directly to Mount Sterling. Mount Sterling's courthouse—in full view of my front porch—had been designated as the central court for the mountain counties in eastern Kentucky, and John Burns was there in court in January 1862.

Sometimes, when I opened the shutters of my Mount Sterling house to let in the cool evening air, I would look down the hill past the former hospital toward the courthouse square and wonder if Frank Mott and John Burns ever crossed paths in Mount Sterling. If they had that January of 1862, neither would know that John Burns was Frank Mott's future father-in-law. Neither would know that Frank Mott would marry Kate Burns—John's favorite child—seven years later in the living room of the fine house John bought for Kizzie Clay, the house that stood across the street from the Catlettsburg courthouse where he served as a judge. Nor would they know that winter during the war that Kate would give birth to the three beauties, who favored John's grandmother Elizabeth Roland, and that the most beautiful, the one who looked most like her grandfather, would be Wynemah—Frank's "Little Indian" and my temperamental but deeply loved grandmother. I only know those things because I bought my house in Mount Sterling.

For years before I moved to Mount Sterling I had wanted to study American history—to understand at least a fraction of what I had learned about Europe as an art historian and manuscript scholar. After I moved to Mount Sterling and, remembering the stories, researched the Clays in chronological order, I began to get a sense of how this country really came together. I learned how lush the soil was in Virginia, how rich the rivers. I saw for the first time how the waterways were indeed the thoroughfares of the seventeenth and eighteenth centuries and that Virginians rarely walked overland to find a bride. I felt more than ever the anger and the frustration the eastern Indian tribes must have experienced as they were driven farther away from their traditional hunting grounds. I did not know until I began my research how long it took to clear enough land to make a living, or how, as communities grew up around a store or a fort, each settler had the responsibility to pay for the upkeep of a road that was part of the town. By following the Clays—and the Cecils and Wittens and the Burns and the Batemans who married into the family—across Virginia and into Kentucky, I learned about a wide swath of America's history.

The Clays are only one family of so many who have the stories to tell that make America come alive from the grassroots up, families who lived through the droughts and floods, the wars and peace, and the political unrest this country has experienced from its beginning in the early seventeenth century to where we are now, four hundred years later. I am blessed to have boxes and drawers full of papers and pictures to help me give form to my family's lives. And the oral history, the wisps of stories that came back to me in Mount Sterling. It was there in that peaceful town in Clay country that my family found me.

I have seen history in a different light over the last few years. I also have discovered something more personal. One night I was walking in Mount Sterling. It was nearly nine o'clock, but in late June the mountains toward the east still hold the reflected glow of the sunset. There was something about the light that stopped me, a fullness I knew from somewhere deep inside. And the air was soft and slightly moist. It wrapped around me the way it used to do when Dick and I chased lightning bugs under the persimmon and plum trees in Old Orchard.

I stopped walking and simply stood there, just feeling Kentucky. And I knew then that despite it all—my running away, my denial of family, my disregard for the stories—Kentucky was my center. I recognized that when I made the decision to approach my family on my own terms, when I chose to treat the stories objectively as clues in historical research, I actually had done something intensely personal. I had taken the first step toward healing the breach about the Clays that existed between Mother and me. And now, as I wrap up my search, I wish Catharine were still alive so that when she asked me once again, "How can you be a historian and not care about your own family?" I could answer, "I do care, Mother, I do. I care in more ways than either of us would ever have imagined."

ACKNOWLEDGMENTS

THREE LIBRARIES were instrumental in providing the information for this book. First is the Mount Sterling–Montgomery County Public Library in Mount Sterling, Kentucky, where the librarian let me search through a drawer of file folders for information on the Clays of Kentucky. The Library of Virginia's online data bank was invaluable for viewing copies of war records, census reports, and other corroborative material. My major source for documents, however, was the Newberry Library in Chicago. For months runners searched for, then carried, stacks of volumes to the long table I had made my own. It was there in the Newberry Library that the early history of my family and of this country came to life for me. And it was there in the library's extensive map collection that I magically saw for the first time the map of Maryland made by Thomas Cecil II, my grandfather eleven generations back.

Many people read for me early on. Irene Tiersten, a writer and my dear friend from graduate school days in Ann Arbor, read the first two drafts of the book and gave incisive suggestions. Julia Kramer and Kathleen Carpenter read early chapters. Julia suggested ways to control the vast genealogy material I was collecting, while Kathleen recommended that I search for the strength of the women in the family. Finally, Joyce Neimanas, a former colleague and neighbor and ongoing close friend, and her mother, June Adduci, gave me the encouragement I needed to keep writing when my spirits flagged. The two of them waited for new chapters each time I visited their home in New Mexico, and in their anticipation and continuing interest assured me that one family's story could be a topic of broader historical interest.

Three people at Chicago Review Press have brought my manuscript to life. Linda Matthews, director, Chicago Review Press, Inc., and Independent Publishers Group, has read for me, guided me, and urged me on when I slowed down. Cynthia Sherry, publisher, took the book under her wing and did everything possible to give it a good sendoff. Plus, she matched me up with Lisa Reardon, editor, who read with a fresh set of eyes. Lisa pointed out where I needed to expand or contract and helped me when I was too close to the material to edit for myself. I am grateful to each of them.

Richard Loving, artist and partner, cooked for me in Mount Sterling while I wrote, told me when it was time to take a break, and never gave up on talking to me despite my frequent looks of abstraction as I continued to compose passages of the family's saga in my head. For those things I am the most grateful.

Notes and Sources

1: The Ancient Planter

The primary sources for the Clay and Cecil families, and for those who married into the family, are county records. These records list land patents, deeds, and wills as well as dates of births, marriages, and deaths. Census rolls are also invaluable as they record the various generations of the family with ages of children and sometimes include a list of personal belongings. The Library of Virginia (LVA) is an excellent source for muster records for the wars fought during the colonial period and the Civil War. The LVA online catalog (www.lva.lib.va.us) links names to wars and includes the counties the soldiers represented, the names of their commanding officers, and photocopies of the muster records.

It should be noted that county designations can be confusing. As the population of the Virginia colony increased, the Virginia Company—and then the Crown—added and renamed counties. In 1634 Henrico County was described as extending from Charles City County "indefinitely westward." Later, Goochland County and Chesterfield County were carved out of Henrico, with more subdivisions to come. These land additions and divisions often took place during a single generation, making deed searches and military records sometimes perplexing.

Three editions of the muster rolls of Virginia's first colonizers provide important information: John Camden Hotten, editor, *The Original Lists of Persons of Quality; Emigrants; Religious Exiles; Political Rebels; Serving Men Sold for a Term of Years; Apprentices; Children Stolen; Maidens Pressed; and Others Who Went from Great Britain to the American Plantations; 1600–1700; With Their Ages, the Localities where they Formerly Lived in the Mother Country, the Names of the Ships in which they Embarked, and other Interesting Particulars. From Mss. Preserved in the State Paper Department of Her Majesty's Public Record Office, England*, Baltimore: Genealogical Publishing Co., 1962; Annie Lash Jester, editor, *Adventurers of Purse and Person: Virginia 1607–1625*, published by The Order of First Families of Virginia, 1607–1624/25, 1957; and Virginia M. Meyer and John Frederick Dorman, editors, *Adventurers of Purse and Person: Virginia 1607–1624/25*, published by The Order of First Families of Virginia, 1607–1624/25, 1987. Jester's edition includes the personal belongings of each of the families counted in the muster rolls of 1624; the other two editions do not. Also an important source for the early generations of Clays in Virginia is Nell Marion Nugent, *Cavaliers and Pioneers: Abstracts of Virginia Land Patents and Grants 1623–1800*, Richmond, VA, 1934; reprinted in Baltimore, MD: Genealogical Publishing Co., 1983. Nugent takes her data from Virginia Patent Books I through V to piece together information on approximately 20,000 early immigrants.

Secondary sources, which include the Clays and Cecils and the later generations of the family, are also useful but must be carefully corroborated with available primary documents. Some of the most helpful are the following: Zachary F. Smith and Mary Rogers Clay, *The Clay Family*, The Filson Club Publications, XIV, Louisville, KY, 1899; David E. Johnston, *A History of the Middle New River Settlements and Contiguous Territory*, Radford, VA: Commonwealth Press, 1906 (online at www.kinyon.com); William C. Pendleton, *History of Tazewell County and Southwest Virginia, 1748–1920*, Richmond, VA: W. C. Hill Printing Company, 1920; William C. Kozee, *Early Families of Eastern and Southeastern Kentucky and Their Descendants*, Baltimore, MD: Genealogical Publishing Co.; William Ely, *The Big Sandy Valley: History of the People and Country from the Earliest Settlement to the Present Time*, Catlettsburg, KY, 1887.

Historical magazines and journals are also useful resources, e.g., William and Mary College, *Quarterly Historical Magazine* and *The Virginia Genealogist.*

Family genealogies have burgeoned online. These "family trees" can give clues but must be viewed with caution as some are more accurate than others. Two of the most popular starting points can be found at www.ancestry.com and www.familysearch.org.

Finally, multitudes of books have been written on America's colonial history. Two I have found useful for background on the colonization of America and on the early phase of the family's history in Virginia and Maryland are Bernard Bailyn, *Voyagers to the West: A Passage in the Peopling of America on the Eve of the Revolution,* New York: Random House, 1986; and David Hackett Fischer, *Albion's Seed: Four British Folkways in America,* New York and Oxford: Oxford University Press, 1989.

A note regarding dates: In 1752 the New (Gregorian) Calendar was adopted in Great Britain, replacing the Old (Julian) Calendar. Early historical sources often are listed with two dates, e.g., March 1623/24, especially during the months of January, February, and March.

Manuscripts recording the workings of the Virginia Company were once owned by Thomas Jefferson and are now in the Library of Congress. A printed version is available: *Records of the Virginia Company,* edited by Susan Myra Kingsbury. Washington, DC: Government Printing Office, vols. I and II, 1906; vols. III and IV, 1933, 1935. See also the Library of Congress abstracts of other primary documents owned by Jefferson online at memory.loc.gov/ammem/collections/jefferson_papers.

Corporate sponsors of the Virginia Company—or "The Tresorer and Companie of Adventurers and Planters of the Citty of London for the Firste Colonie in Virginia," as it was named in its founding documents of 1606—decided that the potential riches of Virginia were worth a third attempt to form a colony on America's Atlantic coast. Although the first two attempts to colonize Virginia by Sir Walter Raleigh had failed, those settlements had private and, consequently, limited backing. For this third try, the stockholders of the Virginia Company—659 in all—would share the costs of seeding the young colony. The return of the investment for the "adventurers"—as the investors called themselves in their corporate charter—

would come from saleable commodities such as lumber and furs that would fill the holds on the return trip of the ships that supplied the colony. The first group of adventurers left London on Friday, December 16, 1606. There were 150 of them on three ships—the *Susan Constant,* the *Godspeed,* and the *Discovery.* They sailed into the Chesapeake Bay on April 26, 1607.

For an overview of Jamestown during John Thomas Claye's early years, including detailed information on Pocahontas, her father, Powhatan, and her husband, John Rolfe, two recent books provide a comprehensive historical and archaeological analysis of the colony: James Horn, *A Land as God Made It: Jamestown and the Birth of America,* New York: Perseus Books Group, 2005; and William M. Kelso, *Jamestown: The Buried Truth,* Charlottesville, VA, and London: University of Virginia Press, 2006. For a primary source on the period, see John Rolfe, *A True Relation of the State of Virginia Lefte by Sir Thomas Dale Knight in May Last 1616,* Charlottesville, VA: University of Virginia Press, 1951.

In 1619 John Thomas became the official owner of his land in Charles City County. In May he paid for the passage of his servant William Nicholls to come over on the ship *Dutie.* William was twenty-six and part of a wave of indentured servants brought over after 1619 by the ancient planters to provide assistance with claiming and planting their newly gained land holdings. The records for a portion of John Thomas Claye's land holdings can be found in the Colony's early Patent Book 1, pp. 230, 404, 432.

On July 13, 1635, John Thomas patented 1,200 acres on Ward's Creek—100 owed him as an "ancient planter" and 1,100 due him for transporting twenty-two persons to the colony. See Patent Book 1, p. 230. He also owned 1,000 acres of land that adjoined his land on Ward's Creek, land that by then was called Clay's Clossett. His land purchases did not stop there. He also owned and sold land on the north side of the James River near Westover, described in a patent granted in 1636 and 1637. See Patent Book 1, pp. 404 and 432.

William Clay, John Thomas's son who lived in Westover Parish, inherited Clay's Closett, which he sold in pieces in 1655 following his father's death. See Charles City County Order Book, 1655–65, p. 245. William Clay was sworn in as constable of Weyanoke Parish in Henrico County in February 1659. He died four years later. I found no records for Thomas and Francis Clay.

2: The Chyrurgien and the Rebel

Bacon's Rebellion has been well documented. The major primary source for the rebellion is located in London in the British Public Record Office, Colonial Office, Class I. Reprinted versions of documents in the British Public Record Office are published by various journals, including *The Virginia Magazine of History and Biography*, 20 (1912), pp. 243ff. or *The William and Mary Quarterly*, 3rd Series, 14 (1957), pp. 403–13. Charles M. Andrews, ed., *Narratives of the Insurrections 1675–1690*, New York, 1915, prints a contemporary account of the rebellion: "A True Narrative of The Rise, Progresse, and Cessation of the Late Rebellion in Virginia." Another personal account, "An Account of Our Late Troubles in Virginia. Written in 1676, By Mrs. An. Cotton, Of Q. Creeke," from the British Public Record Office, Colonial Office, Class I, folios 37 and 38, is reprinted in *The Virginia Magazine of History and Biography*, I (1893), p. 185. The most interesting account of the rebellion is written by Bacon's wife, Elizabeth Duke Bacon, in a letter sent to her sister July 29, 1676, received September 16, 1676: William and Mary College, *Quarterly Historical Magazine*, vol. IX, No. 1, July, 1900, pp. 4ff. (from Eggleston MSS 2395, fol. 550, in the British Public Record Office in London).

For a selected list of secondary sources on the rebellion, see Bernard Bailyn, "Politics and Social Structure in Virginia," in Morton Smith, ed., *Seventeenth Century America*, Chapel Hill: University of North Carolina, 1989; Wilcomb E. Washburn, *The Governor and the Rebel: A History of Bacon's Rebellion in Virginia*, Chapel Hill: University of North Carolina, 1957; and Stephen Sanders Webb, *1676: The End of American Independence*, New York: Knopf, 1984.

The source for a birth date for Charles Clay can be found in the deposition given on October 2, 1682, in which Charles states his age as "about 37 years old": Henrico County, Virginia, Wills and Administrations, Part I: 1677–1692, Will and Deed Book, p. 240. Regarding the gift of two ewes made to Charles Clay on October 3, 1660, by John Wall to his "sonne-in-law Charles Clay," see *Virginia Colonial Abstracts*, Vol. 11, Charles City County Court Orders, 1658–61, p. 78. A court record of Charles Clay's apprenticeship to Stephen Tickner is found in Surry County, Virginia, Court Records 1652–1663, Book I, p. 109.

Hannah Wilson Clay came from an early colonizing family. For reference to her father, John Wilson, see "Lists of the Livinge & the Dead in Virginia, February 16, 1623," *Colonial Records of Virginia*, Richmond, VA: R. F. Walker, Superintendent of Public Printing, 1874, pp. 37–66.

For records of Charles Clay's later life and his estate, see Henrico County, Virginia, Wills and Administrations, Part I: 1677–1692, Will and Deed Book, p. 360: "Charles Clay acquits John Wilson administrator my wife's brother of all claim in above estate. 1 April 1686"; p. 368: "Charles Clay died intestate and his wife Hannah Clay is appointed Adm'x 1 June 1686"; p. 378: Inventory of Charles Clay appraised 15 June 1686. Value: 9392 lbs tobacco. By George Worsham, Godfrey Ragsdale, Nicholas Dison. See also Henrico County, Virginia, Wills and Deeds 1688–1697, Book 3, p. 8: "Accounts of estate of Charles Clay, dec'd, paid by Hannah Clay, his widow and Adm'x. Value 6335 lbs tobacco. Recorded 12 Oct 1688."

For records of Hannah Wilson Clay's later life and her marriage to Edward Stanley, see Henrico County, Virginia, Order Book 1694–1701, p. 106: "Hannah the wife of Edward Stanley took up a servant girl of Mr. Richard Bland." The Westover Plantation was owned by the Blands. Hannah Wilson Clay Stanley died sometime before August 20, 1706, when Edward Stanley was ordered "to bring the remaining orphans of Charles Clay to the next Court to discharge the securities of their estates." See Henrico County, Virginia, Orphans Court Book 1677–1739, p. 47. Also, one of the witnesses of Edward Stanley's will was Henry Clay: Henrico County, Virginia, Wills and Deeds, 1725–37, p. 30.

3: Family Reunion

According to family lore, Green Clay, Mary and Henry's grandson, was urged by his children to write down the Clay family history as he knew it. It is he who tells of Henry's death and where he is buried. A copy of the nine-page handwritten document is on file at the Library of Virginia: Clay Family, *Genealogical Notes*, Accession #32301.

Henry Clay is buried in the small family cemetery about ten miles from Richmond on the road to Amelia. His is the only stone marked. The small cemetery is on Route 360 near Swift Creek.

Source for Henry Clay's will that describes his landholdings: Henrico County, Virginia, Will Book #2, pp. 244–247.

The account of the court proceedings against the grandchildren of Henry Clay is published in an article edited by Peggy Carswell Peacock: "Choctaws in Virginia in 1712! An Adventure 'Beyond Carolina' Taken from Virginia General Court Records," in *The Virginia Genealogist*, Volume 29, Number 1, 1985, pp. 3–8.

4: Mysteries

The indenture between William and Martha Clay and Mathew Moseley was filed on January 21, 1764, in Cumberland County, Virginia: Deed Book #3, pp. 459–461.

The notice posted by a William Clay was published in *The Virginia Gazette*, September 22, 1768, p. 2.

Dunmore's War is discussed in most American histories. Two sources that are particularly descriptive are those found in Alexander Scott Withers, *Chronicles of Border Warfare*, ed. Reuben Gold Thwaites, Cincinnati, OH: R. Clarke Co., 1895, pp. 165–167; and Allan W. Eckert, *That Dark and Bloody River: Chronicles of the Ohio River Valley*, New York: Bantam Books, 1995, pp. 75–96.

Selected sources for Cassius Clay: In 1886 Cassius Clay published his memoir: Cassius Marcellus Clay, *The Life of Cassius Marcellus Clay: Memoirs, Writings, and Speeches*, vol. 1, Cincinnati, OH: J. Fletcher Brennan & Company, 1886. For secondary sources, see H. Edward Richardson, *Cassius Marcellus Clay: Firebrand of Freedom*, Lexington, KY: The University Press of Kentucky, 1976; Carolyn L. Siegel, *Cassius Marcellus Clay: The Man Behind the Legend*, Berea, KY: Kentucky Imprints, 1988; and William H. Townsend, *The Lion of White Hall*, Norman S. Berg, Dunwoody, Georgia, 1967. Account of the happenings on November 14, 1894, is from Townsend, *The Lion of White Hall*, pp. 42ff.

Henry Clay is widely discussed in books and articles. Two early sources for primary documents are edited by Calvin Colton: *The Private Correspondence of Henry Clay*, Cincinnati, OH, 1856; and *The Works of Henry Clay*, New York, 1857, 6 volumes. The Clay Papers Project at the University of Kentucky has collected copies of all of the primary material on Henry Clay and has published the majority of the data in the first ten volumes of *The Papers of Henry Clay*, James F. Hopkins and others, editors, Lexington, KY, 1959–. A major secondary source on Henry Clay, soundly based on primary documents, is Robert V. Remini, *Henry Clay: Statesman for the Union*, New York: W. W. Norton & Company, 1991. Besides an excellent bibliography on Henry Clay, the book contains engraved and photographic images of the various stages of the statesman's life.

5: Family Secrets

For background information on the early settlements along the New River, including the structures of the family groups that moved to the south-western portions of Virginia, see Paula Hathaway Anderson-Green, "The New River Frontier Settlement on the Virginia–North Carolina Border 1760–1820," *Virginia Magazine of History and Biography*, Vol. 86 (1978), pp. 413–431. David E. Johnston, *A History of the Middle New River Settlements and Contiguous Territory*, Huntington, WV: Standard PTG. & Pub. Co., 1906, provides a comprehensive account of the counties in southwest Virginia. In the late nineteenth century Johnston gathered stories from members of the families who settled the region. He includes accounts of the early land purchases and related stories of the Clays, the Belchers, the Baileys, the Cecils, and the Wittens. Johnston's book can be accessed online at www.kinyon.com/westvirginia/midnewriver.html.

For information on the tobacco economy in the mid-eighteenth century, see T. H. Breen, *Tobacco Culture: The Mentality of the Great Tidewater Planters on the Eve of Revolution*, Princeton, NJ: Princeton University, 1985.

In 1765 William Mitchell Clay purchased land in Bedford County from William Mead. The indenture was registered on May 24, 1768, in Bedford County, Virginia: Deed Book #3, p. 159. On July 23, 1770, William Senior sold land to William Junior registered in Bedford County, Virginia: Deed Book #4 1771–1773, p. 98ff. Other indentures between William Mitchell and his sons can be found in Pittsylvania County, Virginia, Deed Book #2 1770–1772.

Mitchell Clay's land on the Bluestone River had originally been assigned to Lieutenant John Draper for his service in the French and Indian War. In exchange for assigning the tract to Mitchell Clay, Draper received from Clay a black slave woman and her children. A copy of the terms of the grant is on file in the Mercer County, West Virginia, county clerk's office. The land is described in Lewis Preston Summers, *History of*

Southwest Virginia, 1746–1786, Washington County, 1777–1870, Richmond, VA, 1903, p. 146: Table titled "Notable Tracts of Land, Surveyed by John Floyd, Hancock Taylor and James Douglas, in 1774–1775, lying mostly in Kentucky": "april 25, 1774 Mitchell Clay 1000 acres both sides Bluestone Cr., Clover Bottom."

Source for Mitchell Clay's will: Giles County, Court Records, Giles County, Wills, pp. 71–73.

6: The Voice

Selected sources on the Cecil and Witten families: David E. Johnston, *A History of the Middle New River Settlements and Contiguous Territory*, Huntington, WV: Standard PTG. & Pub. Co., 1906; William C. Pendleton, *History of Tazewell County and Southwest Virginia, 1748–1920*, Richmond, VA: W. C. Hill Printing Company, 1920; William C. Kozee, *Early Families of Eastern and Southeastern Kentucky and Their Descendants*, Baltimore, MD: Genealogical Publishing Co.

William Clay and Rebecca Cecil were married on April 1, 1800. See Wills and Marriages in Montgomery and Fincastle Counties, Virginia, p. 12. See also ibid., p. 46, which lists the probation of John Cecil's will, Rebecca Cecil Clay's father, in September 1830, which names "wife, Keziah; and children, Philip, Keziah Eaton, Nancy Crandall, Rebeckah Clay, Jenny Grennup, Ricy Satfford, and Betsey Louther, deceased."

Regarding William Clay, see Lewis Preston Summers, *History of Southwest Virginia, 1746–1786, Washington County, 1777–1870*, Richmond, VA: 1903, pp. 873, 875. On November 6, 1798, William Clay was appointed Constable in Captain McComas's Company. On June 4, 1799, Mitchell Clay was recommended as Captain in the 2nd Battalion, 86th Regiment, Charles Clay as Lieutenant and William Clay as Ensign.

William Clay is listed in the Louisa, Kentucky, census of 1840.

7: House Stories

For an overview of the Burns family in Virginia and Kentucky, see William Ely, *The Big Sandy Valley: History of the People and Country from the Earliest Settlement to the Present Time*, Catlettsburg, KY, 1887, pp. 115–118.

Two primary sources documenting James A. Garfield's activities during the Civil War and the Battle of Middle Creek include letters and missives written during his stay in Kizzie Clay's house in Prestonsburg. The first is in a collection of documents: *The War of the Rebellion*, Ser. 1, vol. 10, pt. 2, p. 68, which he directs to the "citizens of the Sandy Valley." The second, in which Garfield recounts the rain before the battle and the deep mud during the fray, is found in Theodore Clark Smith, *The Life and Letters of JA Garfield*, New Haven, CT, 1925, vol. 1, p. 189.

Most of the material on Kizzie Clay is taken from the family's private archives, including diaries, letters, notebooks, photographs, and memorabilia, as well as from oral history.

8: Daddy's Girl

Most of the material on Kate Burns is taken from the family's private archives, including diaries, letters, notebooks, photographs, and memorabilia, as well as from oral history.

John Mavity Burns's career is chronicled by William Ely, *The Big Sandy Valley: History of the People and Country from the Earliest Settlement to the Present Time*, Catlettsburg, KY, 1887, pp. 483–485.

9: Strong Women

Most of the material for this chapter is taken from the family's private archives, including diaries, letters, notebooks, photographs, and memorabilia, as well as from oral history.

The description of Elizabeth Roland is found in William Ely, *The Big Sandy Valley: History of the People and Country from the Earliest Settlement to the Present Time*, Catlettsburg, KY, 1887, p. 115.

Although there are many books available on the interpretation of myths and symbols, my favorite is still *Myths, Rites, Symbols: A Mircea Eliade Reader*, Wendell C. Beane and William G. Doty, editors, New York: Harper & Row, 1975.

10: Little Dolly Dumpling

Most of the material for this chapter is taken from the family's private archives, including diaries, letters, notebooks, photographs, and memorabilia, as well as from oral history.

The History of the Henry Wood's Sons Company Paint Factory, including photographs and the company's logo, can be found on a Wellesley College online site: www.wellesley.edu/Chemistry/PSP/history.html.

11: The Little Indian

Most of the material for this chapter is taken from the family's private archives, including diaries, letters, notebooks, photographs, and memorabilia, as well as from oral history.

The information on the Meinharts was gathered by Mark Meinhart of Pomeroy, Ohio, and handed out to the members of the family.

12: Catharine and Robert

Most of the material for this chapter is taken from the family's private archives, including diaries, letters, notebooks, photographs, and memorabilia, as well as from oral history.

The Bateman side of the family is well documented. My information is taken from personal papers gathered by Richard Bateman Miller, my father's first cousin, and by a published history of the Backenstoe family: Elwood Bruce Backensto, editor, *Backenstoss Family Association of America*, Woodbury, NJ: Gateway Graphics, 1972, and updated on a regular basis.

Census records for Washington Court House and Middletown, Ohio, provide data regarding the number of children and in-laws and their ages who are living in particular households; e.g., both Frank and Ada lived at the home of their father, Clement Bateman, well into their twenties and continued to do so after their marriages.

The obituaries for each of the Highland children were published by the *Washington Register* out of Washington Courthouse, Ohio.

13: Granddaughters

Most of the material for this chapter is taken from the family's private archives, including diaries, letters, notebooks, photographs, and memorabilia, as well as from oral history.

14: House Lust

Most of the material for this chapter is taken from the family's private archives, including diaries, letters, notebooks, t, and memorabilia, as well as from oral history.

15: Kentucky My Way

Information on Mount Sterling, Kentucky, can be found online at www. MtSterlingtourism.com. The site includes photographs of Civil War historical markers plus views of the original downtown.

INDEX